STRONG
LIFE SKILLS

SKILLS FOR WORK AND LIVING
THAT LEAD TO SUCCESS

Jim Clements

DEDICATION

This book is dedicated to my wife and kids, who inspire me to keep pursuing my mission every day.

CONTENTS

ACKNOWLEDGMENTS

So many wonderful people helped make this book a reality. I'd like to thank the following individuals who gave of their time to comb through early drafts of this book to ensure that the material was valid and factual, and provided me with feedback to make it better: Janey Ulmer, Jose Santa-Maria, Elizabeth Dodd, Eric Kaplan, Dr. Kristin Reed, Guillermo Rosas, Sandra Schehl, and Patricia Duff. Of course, I must thank my editor, Jennifer Slater, who went word-by-word through this book to ensure that what you read is the best it can be. I'd like to recognize Bill Martin, Tim Smith, and Lavaaron Davis, three of my personal mentors who taught me most of what I know about a positive work ethic. I would also like to thank the many supporters of my nonprofit, Made New Makerspace, for their encouragement to develop this program into book form. Finally, I want to thank the many young men and women who have taken STRONG life skill workshops throughout the years. Your success from following this program is the reason a book was born in the first place.

Introduction
Adulting is hard

I distinctly recall the first time car trouble left me stuck on the side of the road. I was 17 years old and the proud owner of an ironically named 1983 Plymouth Reliant. It was my first car. I had purchased it for $400, money that I had saved while serving sub sandwiches at my first job.

As a teenager, I took a lot of pride in that rolling disaster of a car. Mismatched interior pieces, a fender and front bumper from a similar model (but not identical) vehicle, a strange musty smell that I never managed to identify or rectify in my entire ownership. You name it, this car had issues with it. Like many teenagers with their first car, however, I saw my Reliant as the greatest thing on four wheels, and I drove it proudly.

Pride can be difficult to overcome, but one great way to do it is to make someone question the source of their pride. This is exactly the position I found myself in as I slowly melted in my dead car on the side of the road, during the afternoon of the hottest day of a midwestern August.

It was miserable. I didn't have air conditioning. My car wouldn't start. I had no clue what was wrong. Sitting there with cars honking and swerving around me on the busy road, I didn't even know what my next step should be. It was one of the worst experiences in my teenage life.

Fortunately, a few minutes after this saga began, it came to an enlightening end. A police officer pulled up behind me and came to see what the problem was. When I explained what happened, she told me to pop the hood and asked me to come with her.

Once we were both in front of the car, the officer propped the hood open and told me to take the air cleaner off the carburetor. She explained that in this hot weather, carbureted vehicles experience something called "vapor lock," where the engine's heat evaporates the gas before it can reach the engine. With the hood open and the carburetor exposed to the outside air, we went back to her police cruiser to wait in the air conditioning until the engine had time to cool. A short while later, with the officer's guidance, I started it back up and made my way home.

While modern fuel injection systems may ensure you never find yourself dealing with vapor lock, at some point in life you'll almost certainly deal with a breakdown. Somewhere out there in America, a flat tire happens every seven seconds, and statistics show that adults who drive will, on average, experience five flat tires in their life. If you drive, it will happen to you.

I want to make something perfectly clear here: it's good to learn to change a tire, but that alone is just one skill. There are thousands of other parts that can fail in a modern car, and unless you're a mechanic, it's unlikely you'll learn how to deal with every one of those problems.

So while it's good to learn solutions to common problems, what will truly help you is learning how to be a problem-solver. You need to learn how to find solutions when you may not know the answers. This isn't just applicable to cars but to all areas of life. Independent problem-solving is truly the secret to "adulting" like a pro.

Introduction

The purpose of this book is to give you the basic tools you need to succeed. You'll learn skills to experience success in the workplace, no matter what your job looks like, as well as in your personal life. Together, these skills will help you succeed in the chaos known as adulthood.

First, we'll lay the foundation with the three things everyone needs – a mission, a mentor, and a mentality. Then you'll learn a six-part program called STRONG. STRONG is an acronym for Safety, Teamwork, Reliability, Orderliness, Noticing, and Growing. It's a set of skills you need to be successful in the workplace (and your personal life) no matter where your life leads. Finally, we'll put the pieces together and help you develop a winning strategy for your future. Throughout the book, you will find useful tips on solving the problems that are guaranteed to come your way.

Life isn't always going to be perfect. Nobody succeeds at everything. Even equipped with all the tools in this book, you'll encounter setbacks and trials along the path. Don't be discouraged – this happens to everyone. The objective of this book isn't to make your life perfect; it's to give you the best chances at overall success even when faced with momentary failures.

Adulthood is an adventure, and with the skills in this book, it's an adventure you'll be prepared to take on!

4

Part I:
A foundation for success

Chapter 1 –
You need a mission

Success doesn't come easy

Odds are pretty good that you've been told success doesn't come easy. In contrast, however, our society is filled with people who seemingly came upon easy success. Look no further than your favorite social media platform and you'll find influencers who seem to party every day, getting rewarded with millions of fans and piles of money.

Sometimes the influencer phenomenon leads us to think that success is a simple formula. Do something that gets attention, post it online, and in no time, you'll have a massive following and make your living as an influencer on YouTube or TikTok or the next big thing. The only problem with this formula is that it's not reality.

While many influencers make their social media accounts appear as though they're random off-the-cuff fun, this couldn't be further from the truth. Virtually all of the major social media influencers have entire staffs – producers, editors, and writers, all working hard to create the illusion of spontaneous fun. Even when they were just getting started, many were already investing tens of thousands of dollars into their channels while working on them several hours a day. In other words, their success didn't come easy.

Does the reality that success doesn't come easy mean success is unattainable? Should we give up and quit trying to make something of our lives because this sort of success is hard? No way! In fact, the entire purpose of this book is to help you make your life a success story. In its pages are tips and tricks derived from people who have become successful, along with a breakdown of the skills that you need to solve problems and write your success story. If you read along and take the lessons in this book to heart, you can experience success.

Success isn't always riches and fame

Becoming an online star is one form of success, but it's far from the only one. If you look up "success" in the Oxford Dictionary, this is how it's defined:

"The accomplishment of an aim or purpose."

According to that definition, being successful really only requires you to set and accomplish a mission. During that mission, there will be problems that get in the way. These obstacles can be small, or they can be enormous. No matter the size, to address problems on the way to our mission, we set goals. Those goals are stepping stones to success.

The purpose of this book is to help you find success, both in the small day-by-day goals, and also the big, life-sized missions. There are three factors that you must have to get there:

1. A mission – the direction and purpose that you wish to pursue.
2. A mentor – someone with the experiences and knowledge you need to acquire.
3. A mentality – the thoughts and behaviors that will lead to success.

This is your winning formula. If you can put these three factors to work in your life, it will give you direction. It won't always be easy; sometimes the path to success is riddled with difficulty. This is where being a problem-solver will save you. Before we can get to that point, however, the first step is to find the main thing you need: a mission.

What is a mission, anyway?

Most of us already have a picture formed in our mind of what it means to be "on a mission." Some people might see being on a mission as something for a military unit. Others might associate it with religion, such as being a missionary.

In reality, a mission can be *any* assignment to carry out for a significant purpose. Your mission is the compass that guides the direction of your life. In the STRONG program, we define a mission this way:

"An overarching aim or purpose."

Keep this definition in mind, because we'll talk about setting a mission for yourself in a moment. First though, we need to talk about goals.

Gotta have goals

Often, we treat goals and missions as though they are the same thing. They're not! A mission is big. It's an overarching aim or purpose, while a goal is an attainable step that you take to help you ultimately accomplish your mission.

Another way to look at goals is to see them as problem-solving tools. For example, if your mission is to make it through the next school year with all As and Bs, a lack of sleep may create problems. To solve that problem, you set a goal of going to bed at a certain time during the school week.

Goals are a part of your mission. They can be big or small, and typically come in a couple varieties:

1. Short-term goals – These are goals that can usually be accomplished in a moment, a day, or maybe a few days. Some examples of short-term goals are catching up on laundry, cleaning your apartment, or checking the oil in your car. These are things you want to accomplish *right now* or *very soon*.
2. Long-term goals – These goals might take a few days to accomplish on the short end, and can take weeks or a few months to achieve on the long end. Some examples might be buying a car, leasing an apartment, or passing your current semester at school.

Within many long-term goals (and even some short-term goals) you may have other goals. If you had a long-term goal to build your credit score, you may have a short-term goal to sign a lease on an apartment or make all of your payments on time. All of these goals work together toward the long-term goal, and more importantly, toward your mission.

Being SMART with your goals

In 1981 George Duran, a business expert and consultant, coined the term SMART Goals. Much like our own STRONG program, SMART is an acronym that makes it easier to remember how to set goals. Today, when we talk about a SMART goal, that means the goal is:

1. Specific – A specific goal is well defined and identifies what you want to accomplish.
2. Measurable – To be measurable, a goal must be easy to check or evaluate along the way to monitor your progress.
3. Achievable – Your goal must be something actually possible to accomplish.
4. Relevant – A relevant goal will always be in line with your overall mission.
5. Time-bound – While your mission may not always have a specific timeline, goals always need to have a timeframe for completion.

For example, the following could be my own SMART goal: "I will finish writing the first chapter of this book by next Tuesday."

This goal checks off all the boxes. It's specific – I'm going to finish this chapter. It's measurable – I can look at my progress to see how far along I am. It's achievable – This is a realistic timeline. It's relevant – Finishing this chapter fits in my personal mission to use my gifts and abilities to make the world a better place. It's time-bound – I have until next Tuesday to reach my goal.

So if that's a good goal, then what does a bad goal look like? Here's one example: "I'm going to be rich"

This goal is not very SMART. It's not specific – I don't even say how I'm going to become rich. It's not measurable – What is rich? Millionaire? Billionaire? It depends. It's not achievable – When I chose to prioritize starting a non-profit organization and writing a book, I was not choosing a path to wealth. It's not relevant – my mission to make the world a better place has very little to do with whether I'm rich or poor. Finally, it's not time-bound – I never state a time when I intend to be rich, so I can't tell whether I'm on track.

So often, we fail to reach our goals because we don't set the right kind of goals, or we mistake our dreams for goals. Dreams – the wishes we have for our future – are wonderful things. There's nothing wrong with dreaming about where we want to be or who we want to become. Our dreams can even be the basis for goals or our greater mission in life. However, without transforming those dreams into SMART goals, they can't accomplish much good.

If you want to have any hope of accomplishing not only your goals, but the greater mission that drives them, then you must create strong, SMART goals. This is how you set yourself up for success.

Let's practice setting a SMART goal. Think about something you want to accomplish. Then either below or on a separate piece of paper, write out that goal.

My goal:

_____

_____

_____

   After you write out your goal, answer these questions to develop your goal into a SMART goal:

How is it *Specific?*

_____

How is it *Measurable?*

_____

How is it *Achievable?*

_____

How is it *Relevant?*

_____

How is it *Time-bound?*

_____

   Now that you've answered these questions, rewrite your goal to incorporate the SMART goal components below or on a separate sheet of paper:

My goal:

_____

_____

_____

As you develop your mission, keep this goal-setting method close by. You will need to use it over and over. Keep in mind that your overall mission is going to consist of goals of all sizes and that there will be some strategic stacking of smaller goals that help you reach the bigger goals.

Practice setting goals daily

You don't just wake up one day a pro at setting goals and executing them. You have to build those goal-setting muscles. A good habit to build is to set at least one significant short-term goal for yourself every day. By setting these short, attainable goals, you're not only working toward your mission, you're developing a habit of being intentional with your life.

Initially, write out your daily goal, then at the end of the day evaluate how you did. Remember that a good goal is measurable. If you don't accomplish your goal, that's okay as long as you can measure the progress you made and make a plan for what you will do differently next time.

Your mission: more than a goal

Remember the description of a mission from earlier? I described a mission as an assignment you carry out for a significant purpose. We also covered how a mission is different from a goal, in that a mission is a broader concept, where goals are specific objectives to accomplish. Let's take some time to unpack this and really understand a mission from top to bottom.

In your life, a mission is a definition of who you are and where you want to go with your life; it can almost be thought of as a life purpose. By giving yourself a mission, you're declaring who you are and what your purpose is. Like a compass, a good mission will give you a direction to steer toward. It will also help you identify things to avoid. Typically, a person has one mission they're working toward, the purpose that they use to propel themselves.

When we talk about a mission, it's often expressed through a mission statement. A mission statement is simply a tool that spells out our mission in plain language. Having a written mission statement is a huge advantage as it's something you can look at from time to time to evaluate your progress.

Before we write a personal mission statement, let's take a look at the business world. Most businesses have a mission statement they use to help guide their activities. Here are a few examples of real-world business mission statements:

Krispy Kreme Doughnuts: To make the most awesome doughnuts on the planet every single day.

Disney: To entertain, inform and inspire people around the globe through the power of unparalleled storytelling, reflecting the iconic brands, creative minds and innovative technologies that make ours the world's premier entertainment company.

Nike: To bring inspiration and innovation to every athlete* in the world. (*If you have a body, you are an athlete.)

Made New Makerspace: To empower foster and underserved youth for their success in a community that promotes learning, collaboration, and creation.

When you read these mission statements, you can tell exactly what the purpose of each business is. These businesses use their mission statement to drive their services. When you walk into a Krispy Kreme, you can see that they truly want to make the most awesome doughnuts. Disney absolutely delivers the magic they spell out in their mission. Nike's entire brand revolves around their mission. Finally, while Made New Makerspace, the organization I started in 2018, might not be a global brand like the others, its mission statement has been the driving force behind everything we do, including the publication of this very book.

If a business is a good business, they have and follow a mission statement. Likewise, if you want to succeed, you need a personal mission statement.

Do I *really* need a personal mission statement?

At this point, you might be asking if you really need a personal mission statement. The answer to this question is an emphatic YES! A personal mission statement is incredibly useful for helping you find something essential to your life: direction. It can be very easy to get off track. By having a statement that says who you are and what you're about, you're giving yourself a tool to help you keep your life on track, moving toward your goals and ultimately success.

When I talk about the importance of personal mission statements, people often ask if this is something that other people really do. Again, the answer is a great big yes. In fact, many of the most successful people in this world have personal mission statements. Consider these examples:

- Dwayne "The Rock" Johnson: "Be the hardest worker in the room."
- Oprah Winfrey: "To be a teacher. And to be known for inspiring my students to be more than they thought they could be."
- Elon Musk: "If something is important enough you should try, even if the probable outcome is failure."
- Walt Disney: "To make people happy."
- Maya Angelou: "My mission in life is not merely to survive, but to thrive; and to do so with some passion, some compassion, some humor, and some style."

These are great examples, because when you look at these people's lives, you can see that they absolutely live up to their mission. By setting a mission, they gave themselves the direction they needed to find their success.

Ingredients for a good mission statement

Now that we've looked at some corporate and personal mission statements, let's get to work on yours. A good mission statement has these characteristics:

1. Simple: A mission statement doesn't have to be wordy. In fact, it should use the fewest words possible to sum up your mission. Keep your mission short and sweet.
2. Significant: Your mission has to matter to you. This isn't anybody else's mission – it's yours! Make sure your mission aligns with your values, who you are, and what you believe.
3. Success-oriented: A good mission statement sets you up for success by giving you something to push toward and a mark to hold yourself accountable to. It should state what your successful life would look like.

Creating a personal mission statement can take a lot of time to work out. You might find yourself creating a mission statement today that you revise tomorrow. This revision process is part of learning who you are and what you want to be.

The mission statement at Made New Makerspace changed numerous times before our official launch, and we even modified it again after operating for four years, to better reflect what we wanted to be. My own personal mission statement is regularly evolving as I evaluate and adjust it. Don't be afraid to revise your mission!

Here are a few examples of personal mission statements:

- To use my gifts to inspire and motivate others
- To inspire change through teaching
- To treat those I encounter with compassion and love
- To use my gifts of leadership to help others find solutions
You can see that all of these mission statements lay out personal values, give a standard to measure success, and set boundaries. These are great personal mission statements.

But wait a second! What about goals? These mission statements are pretty vague compared to the very specific SMART goals we discussed earlier. How do they all fit? That is a good question to be asking right now.

Remember that a mission is the large, overarching direction for your life, and goals are specific components that help you accomplish your mission and solve the problems that can interfere with it.

For example, if your mission statement was "to inspire change through teaching," you might set a goal to enroll in a teaching program at a local college and become a teacher. Maybe a future goal would be to start an organization that improves the community through offering public education. And within each of these long-term goals, there would also be many short-term goals. All of these goals fit under the umbrella of your overall mission.

Let's take a moment to write out the first draft of your mission statement. I call it a first draft because it's likely that you will need more time to refine your mission, and it will change over time. That's perfectly fine.

Before you write out a mission statement, think about who you are and what you want in your life. Below or on a separate piece of paper, answer the following questions:

What are your values and principles? Which do you feel are most important to you?

As of right now, what is the major direction that you want to orient your life toward?

How do you want to impact the world around you?

Considering these points, put together a mission statement that brings them all together. It can be several sentences long, or just a few words; it just needs to be something that has meaning to YOU and can guide you toward success.

My mission:

Now that you've written out a first draft mission, transfer it to a piece of paper and put it someplace you will see every day. As time passes, make changes to this statement and use it to evaluate how you're doing.

Packing goals into your mission

With your mission statement laid out, it's time to start packing goals into it. Think about some long-term goals that will move you toward your mission. Write these out, then identify and plan the steps you need to reach those goals. These steps will become the shorter-term goals that you set in order to get there. This process will help you become a better problem-solver and ultimately lead to your success.

Side quests

Not everything in our day-to-day lives has to be 100% mission-oriented. "side quests" are a part of all of our lives, and sometimes they're a very necessary distraction. If you did nothing but lay out goals all day, every day, eventually you'd burn out, probably sooner than later.

Intentionally make time in your life for things that aren't strictly mission-related. Maybe this is a vacation. Perhaps you have hobbies or activities that you enjoy. Whatever the case may be, make time for these side quests. As long as they don't dominate your life or undermine your mission, they are a helpful, healthy, necessary part of a successful life.

Putting it all together

Creating a mission for yourself doesn't need to be hard, but it will take time, and more than likely, you will continue to revise your mission over the months and years ahead. By giving yourself a mission, though, you give yourself something incredibly important: a direction toward success.

If you follow your mission, set goals for yourself that are in line with your mission, and keep track of how you're doing, you're laying a firm foundation. And that leads us to the next thing you'll need to reach success: a mentor.

Chapter 2 –
You need a mentor

Your secret weapon

In the first chapter, we learned that it is essential to have a mission to become successful. We also learned about goals and how they are an important part of every mission. As you live out your mission and set goals for your life, there is a secret weapon that will help you along the way: mentors.

What is a mentor?

The Oxford Dictionary defines a mentor like this:

"an experienced and trusted adviser."

In other words, a mentor is someone who can teach you the skills you need to succeed. A mentor can be anyone who has the experience in life that you yourself need. Perhaps this is a pastor at a church or the mechanic at a nearby garage. Maybe it's a classmate who has learned a skill you want to master. Mentors can be anyone as long as they have experience in an area where you need to grow in and you can trust them to help you.

Why mentors matter

It's important to have mentors because life is hard. You can't know everything. We all need people we can call on from time to time to show us the direction to go. By doing this, your mentors will drastically increase your chances of success.

Mentors also help you become a better problem-solver. When you face a difficult situation, a good mentor can talk you through it and help you decide on the best solution. You will learn problem-solving skills by observing and participating, making you a better problem-solver and more successful.

Have you ever held a camera super close to something? If so, you've noticed that the image is too blurry to see the subject. The same thing is true for us. One of the problems we all have when evaluating ourselves is that we're "too close." Because you're you, it's hard for you to step away from your deeply held convictions, beliefs, and perspectives to get a truly objective look at your life. This is another way a relationship with a mentor comes in handy.

Talking with a mentor is useful when you're setting goals for yourself, as we talked about in the first chapter. Sometimes we need another person who can see us from the outside and help us determine what to work toward. Because they can see you from the outside, they may have insight you've never even considered.

Mentors come in all shapes and sizes

If having a mentor is so useful, the next question might be "what does a mentor look like?" Stop for a moment and think about what a mentor looks like to you. Some people see mentoring as a very formal relationship – someone much older than you, maybe a boss or teacher, or someone with whom you have regular, scheduled meetings and evaluations. While this image is true of some mentors, a mentor can really be anybody, as long as they are a trusted advisor with experiences that benefit you. This means a mentor can be older than you – or younger. They can be someone who you work for – or someone who works for you. You can even be the mentor of someone who has mentored you in the past.

Early in my adult life, I had a mentor named Lavaaron, who happened to be one of my managers. As he mentored me, I learned valuable lessons about work ethics that I carry with me to this day. Years later we reconnected, and I had the privilege to be his mentor for a while and help him address certain goals in his personal life.

The point is that just about anyone can be a mentor, and mentoring doesn't need to be a super structured, formal thing either. You might even have mentors in your life right now, and you didn't realize it because you don't call them a mentor. But think about it – is there anyone in your life who you trust, who has given you useful guidance? That's a mentor!

You need multiple mentors

You need more than one mentor in your life. Sometimes there's one main person who you see as a major mentor figure, but even then, you need other "minor" mentors. Nobody knows everything, and someone who makes an excellent mentor in one area might come up short in another.

As a teen, driving my cherished but beat-up Plymouth Reliant, I frequently dealt with car problems. Fortunately, I had a mentor in Tom, who ran the auto repair shop in our neighborhood. Tom would let me bring my car into his shop, and he'd show me what was wrong with it. Usually, he wouldn't charge me but instead teach me how I could fix the problem myself.

With Tom's mentoring, I was able to replace fenders and the front bumper, rebuild the carburetor, and more. Tom made an excellent automotive repair mentor. The guidance he gave me has stuck with me all my life, even as an adult teaching automotive repair classes to high school students.

Another mentor in my teen years was Bill, my supervisor at my maintenance job. Bill helped me understand the importance of having a good work ethic. He was someone who I could always come to with a question and was willing to take time to invest in my development.

While I would go to Tom for my automotive mentoring or Bill for my career mentoring, I also found other mentors skilled in different areas. Thanks to this diverse mentor base, I became a more well-rounded person and better equipped to be successful. This is the value of having multiple mentors.

Finding a mentor

How do you find a mentor? This can be daunting and feel like the challenge that will hold you back. It might seem difficult to find mentors, but the truth is that they're all around you. Again, you may have people in your life who you didn't even realize are already mentors.

The first step to finding a mentor is to understand what you're looking for in a mentor. Do you want someone to help you with figuring out life in general? Are you looking to learn a particular skill? Do you need help doing some self-evaluation or goal-setting? Having a good idea of what you want to get out of a mentoring relationship will help you identify those people who would make natural mentors in your life.

Once you've gone through the process of identifying how you want a mentor to help you grow, the next step is to consider the people in your life who you already know. Remember, anyone can be a mentor. The only criteria they need to have are these:

1. They are trustworthy
2. They have experience that you can learn from
3. They're willing to share their experience

Think about those three criteria and who you know already. Once you've identified a potential mentor, you can decide how you want the mentoring relationship to work.

For some people it's more effective to go up to a person and flat-out ask them to mentor you. You could say something like "Hey friend, I really appreciate your skills in _____. I've been looking to learn more about that, and if you're willing, I'd love to have you mentor me in this. Would you be willing to do that?" Don't be surprised if they have questions about how you envision the mentoring relationship.

This direct approach is great because it makes the mentorship clear. It sets them up for success as a mentor because they can prepare, set aside time, and put thought into mentoring you.

Sometimes, though, mentoring isn't nearly that formal. In fact, you might have mentors who you've never asked to mentor you. If a person is involved with your life already, it might just be natural for them to show you the things you want to learn without you ever specifically asking.

The bottom line is that you really need to have relationships with people in your life who you can trust to learn from, so take those wherever and however you can get them.

Mentors make you a problem-solver

One benefit of having a mentor is that they help you become a better problem-solver. Being able to solve problems is perhaps the single most important part of leading a successful life. By having mentors around you, you can observe how they solve problems and translate their skills into your life.

This means that when you're looking for a mentor, pay attention to how well they solve problems that come up in their life. Do they handle them well? Are they able to come up with ideas to solve their problems? Do they look for help when they need it? If the answers to these questions are "yes," then you may have a good prospective mentor on your hands!

Mentored goals and missions

With mentors in place, you now have a resource to evaluate your personal mission and goals. Take these to your mentors. Ask them what they think. Get input that helps you. More than that, accept at least some of their advice and listen to them.

In Part Two, we'll be talking about STRONG skills to make you a better worker and member of the community. The "G" stands for "Growing," and a big part of growing is learning to accept valid feedback, even if you don't like it.

Sometimes a mentor will tell you things about your plans that you don't like to hear. That doesn't necessarily mean that they're a bad mentor. It might just mean that your plan stinks and needs to change. Learning to accept that sort of feedback isn't easy, but it's a crucial part of growing. It's also important for the next area we're going to cover: you need a mentality.

Chapter 3 –
You need a mentality

The most important part

In the first chapter, we learned about the importance of a personal mission statement and goals. In the second chapter, we discovered that mentors are a key part of your journey to success. Here in the third chapter we're going to cover the final element to establish a foundation for a successful life: your mentality.

How you think and behave are perhaps the most important components of a successful life. You can have the best mission statement ever, along with SMART goals and mentors to help you accomplish them, but without the mentality to start making it happen, you're not going to implement anything. This is why we will cover your mentality not only in this chapter, but in all of Part II as we learn about STRONG.

Think like a success story

One key to becoming a success story is to think like one. That sounds almost overly simplistic, but it really is true. How you think impacts how you feel and how you behave. If you focus on failure, only look at faults, and never give yourself a chance, you are never going to succeed.

So how do you think like a success? Let's start by going back to mentors. Think about the people who you'd like to have as mentors. While you can't read their minds, you can tell a lot about how they think by how they present themselves. Are they positive or negative? Are they problem-solvers? Do they embrace change or push against it?

Learning to emulate the mentality of your mentors is as important as listening to the words they have for you. Their advice is important, of course, but unless you change your thinking and start seeing yourself as capable of success, you won't get there.

Thinking like a success takes time and practice. It's something you have to work toward. There are a number of characteristics that define thinking like a success. Practicing them will lead to living them, and living them will lead to success.

Here are a few characteristics of thinking like a success that you can start working on right now.

Embrace change

You aren't perfect. That's not an insult, it's just a fact. I'm not perfect either. One characteristic of a successful mentality is embracing change. When you're able to embrace change, you're able to grow as a person.

In my 30's I worked as a counselor at a national crisis hotline. When someone is struggling, they can call a hotline and the counselors will help them stay calm and focus on getting through their crisis.

In my time doing this, I worked with hundreds of callers. Many of them were repeat callers who seemed to live in almost constant crisis. Even if we could talk them through a crisis today, they would call back tomorrow in another crisis.

One pattern I noticed in these repeat callers was that they struggled to embrace change. When I offered suggestions to help them to cope with their terrible situations, the answer was often the same: I can't do that.

Sometimes they had excuses for why they couldn't change their situation. Other times they didn't. Either way, they were absolutely resolute: their problem could not be solved. Change could not happen.

When you believe you can't change, you're sealing your fate. For so many of my callers, they could have made small changes in their lives that would have led to a better life. Despite this, they couldn't bring themselves to make changes, and their lives remained miserable.

Often we've built walls in our minds that prevent us from making the changes necessary for success. This is a barrier to problem-solving, and without problem-solving, we won't improve our lives. Sometimes you really can't do something for valid reasons, but don't let that be the end. That just means you need to keep working to find a different solution that you are able to do.

When you feel stuck in life, that usually indicates it's time to take a step back and look whether there's something you need to change. In these times, it's important to be on the lookout for signs of rigid thinking, such as saying "I can't" to a potential solution or refusing to try new ideas to address your problems. Break out of this sort of thinking, and embrace change.

See failure as a gift

We've already covered the fact that you and I aren't perfect. Because we're not perfect, we're going to make mistakes. There are at least three ways we often handle failure in our lives: denying that we failed, getting angry over failure, or embracing failure. Let's explore these.

Denying that we failed

One way we can deal with failure is to actively deny that there was any failure in the first place. This can cause your failures to get worse and worse as time goes by, making you a loose cannon.

In April 1986, Reactor Number Four at Chernobyl went into meltdown. According to the World Nuclear Association, it was and still is the worst nuclear accident in human history. It's also a great example of what can happen when you deny failure. The accident, which was the result of a safety test gone wrong, would have been entirely avoided if the leadership at the plant admitted their failures.

It all began long before the meltdown, when an unexpected delay meant that an unprepared shift of workers would be conducting the safety test. They should have admitted failure and stopped there. But they pressed forward. One failure led to another and another, most of which the leaders ignored. This chain reaction of failures and denials leading to more failures and more denials finally led to a literal nuclear chain reaction and plant meltdown. It spread contamination across the globe that is still affecting people today.

While this is an extreme example, in our day-to-day lives, denying failure can lead to our own personal meltdowns. Though it seems counterintuitive, if you want to succeed, you need to admit when you fail.

Anger over failure

Another way we tend to react to failure is through anger. This can take many forms. Sometimes we're angry at ourselves. Other times, we blame our failure on others. Both are toxic. Just like when we deny failure, reacting to our failures with anger makes it more likely that we will fail again.

That's not to say that we can't feel angry in certain situations. At times, being angry over an outcome is normal and expected. However, when we use anger to deflect blame for our own failures onto others, we miss an opportunity to improve ourselves. Further, when you react in anger to others over your own failure, it builds walls, eliminates mentors, and makes problem-solving more difficult. It serves nobody, especially yourself, because those people will be less available to help you succeed in the future.

Embracing failure

Finally, there's a third – and best – way to react to failure: accept and embrace it. Failure is an important part of the learning process. Through accepting our failures and learning from them, we become better and better people.

This does not mean that failure will feel good. Sometimes it will hurt. Sometimes it will hurt – A LOT. That's okay. We can still work through that hurt and see each failure as the valuable experience it truly is.

Think about learning to ride a bike. How do we learn to do it? We fail, over and over again. A child might fall off their bike a hundred times before they learn to ride it. The secret is to embrace that failure, get back on the bike, and try again.

In fact, learning to ride a bike is really a great analogy for the steps to experiencing success in general. You begin with a mission to learn how to ride a bike. Parents or caregivers are your mentors, helping you with the advice and instruction you need. You set goals along the way like balancing and pedaling while someone holds the bike. Finally, you put everything into practice. You might fall again and again, but if you have the mentality not to give up, you eventually learn to ride your bike, despite all the failures along the way.

Just like falling while learning to ride a bike, failure is a part of life. More than that, failure is a gift, a chance to start over again with more experience. Embrace failure when it happens, get up, dust yourself off, and don't give up.

The power of positivity

Another factor that can make the difference between success and failure is a positive mindset. This isn't just anecdotal: in 2005, researchers studied more than 275,000 people, and found that those who have a positive outlook tend to be healthier, more successful, and steer clear of destructive behaviors. In other words, if you think positively, you're more likely to lead a positive life.

It's one thing to know that a positive outlook is helpful; it's another to actually live it. Sometimes we're so ingrained in our habits and past behaviors that we have difficulty breaking free from negative thinking.

Breaking free begins with self-monitoring. Listen to yourself to be aware of when you're speaking or thinking negatively. When you catch yourself doing it, actively correct yourself with a positive replacement statement or thought. For example, if you catch yourself saying "I can't do this" try correcting that with "I'll give this my best effort." This is a hard habit to build; don't despair if you struggle with it at first.

A positive mentality takes time to develop, but just like riding a bike, if you work on it, you will master it. Like everything else, you'll make more progress overcoming negative thoughts if you set goals to do so and have mentors who can help you.

Gotta have grit

People often overlook one aspect of a success mentality – grit. The Oxford Dictionary defines grit:

"Courage and resolve; strength of character."

To put it another way, you could think of grit as the ability to stick to something and to make it happen no matter what. Having grit means that when things get difficult you don't throw up your hands and walk away. Instead you dig in, press on, and push toward completion.

Any time you move in an intentional direction, whether as part of a goal or a larger mission, you're going to encounter resistance. Things won't always go your way. Roadblocks will stop you in your tracks. When you encounter setbacks, realize that these things are normal, and keep pressing on toward fulfilling your mission.

Be excellent to each other

If there's one characteristic of a successful mentality that would benefit everyone, it's treating others with excellence. In today's social media culture, it can be easy to talk down to others. This leads to strife and will slow you down on your path to success. True leaders and successful people lift others up.

People who are able to treat others with dignity create a culture of camaraderie around them. Others naturally want to be around them, and when they need a hand, they're more likely to find help. Truly, the golden rule – do unto others as you would have them do unto you – is a critical component of a successful mentality.

Be STRONG

Finally, be a person of STRONG character. The next section of this book will go into detail about the STRONG life skills program. There are six components to STRONG: Safety, Teamwork, Reliability, Orderliness, Noticing, and Growing. Each one will help you lead a life of success, not only in the workforce, but in your personal life as well.

Put it all together

You need a mission. You need mentors. You need a mentality. With these three elements, you can succeed. Developing them will take work. Success doesn't come easy, but that doesn't mean it's impossible. Work at it, learn to be STRONG, and the sky's the limit!

Part II:
STRONG skills for success

Chapter 4 –
The STRONG Life Skills

Time to get STRONG

In the first part of this book, we laid a foundation for success through identifying the need for a mission, a mentor, and a mentality. Now it's time to build on that foundation and discover the soft skills you need to achieve success.

What are soft skills? The Oxford Dictionary defines them as:

"personal attributes that enable someone to interact effectively and harmoniously with other people."

In other words, soft skills are the tools that help you deal with the people around you.

Soft skills are different from hard skills. Hard skills are specific job skills needed to complete a task, such as a metalworker learning to use an angle grinder. In contrast, soft skills are the personal qualities you bring with you into a situation, especially the workplace.

The biggest advantage of soft skills over hard skills is that soft skills come with you everywhere you go, and will be useful in every job you have. That angle-grinder knowledge from your metalworking job might not be much use if you switch to an office setting, but a soft skill like being able to accept a supervisor's feedback and grow is a benefit at any job.

Having soft skills, and being able to work effectively with others, is critically important in our society. In 2019, LinkedIn's Global Talent Trends report showed that 92% of hiring managers believed that soft skills were as important – or more important – than hard skills when hiring new staff. Or as a construction manager once told me, "It's a lot easier to teach a kid to hold a saw than it is to teach them to show up on time." This is where STRONG comes into play.

STRONG is a life skill program that teaches the soft skills you need to become a success story. I developed it over five years through researching what employers actually need from their employees. Hundreds of teens and young adults have found success through the program to date.

You CAN learn soft skills

In the process of developing STRONG, I spoke with dozens of different hiring managers and employers to learn the skills they wanted from new employees. I discovered that nearly every employer was looking for soft skills as opposed to hard skills.

It was also during this process, however, that I heard a phrase over and over again from employers: "You can't teach soft skills." This is such a commonly-held belief that it's almost a mantra, especially in the trades. The problem with this mentality is that it's completely false.

The truth is that you *can* learn soft skills. When managers say that soft skills can't be taught, what they usually mean is that they're specialists in teaching the hard skills needed for their occupation, and they don't have the expertise or time to teach soft skills.

This isn't necessarily a bad thing. Managers should be specialists in teaching the hard skills needed for their occupation. However, to learn soft skills, you need to find a teacher or program that specializes in soft skill development. That's exactly the foundation on which I built STRONG.

How to learn STRONG life skills

STRONG sorts dozens of soft skills into six topics – Safety, Teamwork, Reliability, Orderliness, Noticing, and Growing. Within each of these topics are individual skills that will benefit you in the workplace and beyond.

Over the next six chapters we'll look at each component of STRONG. In each chapter you'll find sections that break down that component of STRONG. You'll also occasionally find questions that someone who is practicing that skill may ask.

One question you may have right now is "Who is STRONG for?" The short answer is *everyone*. While this book was written primarily for young adults learning skills for the workforce, STRONG is a set of skills that can benefit anyone. If you're reading this book, you can benefit from learning STRONG.

I recommend that you work through each chapter of STRONG one at a time. As you go, have a place to take notes – extra sheet of paper, notebook, phone app, or whatever works best for you. In these notes, write out how each topic ties into what you are currently doing, whether as an employee or a student. Then write out why you think each topic or subtopic is important to employers. This not only helps you understand STRONG and soft skills in general, but it will give you valuable insight that will lead to your own success, both as an employee and as a leader.

You can learn to succeed in the workplace and beyond. STRONG can help you get there. Read on through the next six chapters, and get ready to get STRONG!

Chapter 5 –
Safety

Being STRONG starts with Safety

First steps are important. They define us. Nobody talks about a baby taking their second step – it's always that first step that matters. Everyone knows Neil Armstrong took the first step on the moon, but unless you're an astronomy geek you probably can't name the fifth person to accomplish that feat. First steps are a big deal, and that's why STRONG starts with Safety.

When I was first developing STRONG life skills, I went through dozens of iterations looking for the best way to explain the soft skills that lead to success. Early on, I realized that no matter what the program looked like, occupational safety had to lead the way.

The same can be said for your personal safety. You can be a great person in every measurable way, but if you don't have a safety-focused mindset, you open the door to being victimized by the dangers of the world. Those dangers are real, they will prevent you from reaching success, and they can be painful.

Why is safety so important for being successful? The short answer is that unsafe people tend to become victims of their behavior. If you don't take safety seriously, your odds of coming into calamity are far greater.

A tendency toward unsafe behavior also stifles your opportunities for growth and advancement in the workplace. At work, you might have the best customer service skills in the company, but if you regularly put yourself, your coworkers, or your customers into dangerous situations you probably won't last long in that position.

Safety isn't always about physical dangers, either. Some dangers won't physically injure you, but can still leave you hurt. In my early 20s, I was the victim of check fraud. Physically, I was uninjured, but the mental and moral injuries of that financial harm still sting.

Everything in moderation

While safety is our first step in being STRONG, it's not our only step. Yes, we want to lead safe lives. Absolutely, workplace safety needs to be a focus when we're on the job. But we also need to recognize that at the end of the day, if we get so wrapped up in safety that we can't function, we've gone overboard.

TV host and skilled labor advocate Mike Rowe developed a slogan several years ago on his show Dirty Jobs, called "Safety Third." The point of this slogan was not to minimize safety, but to help his crew put safety into context.

Mike Rowe's "Safety Third" mentality is based on the notion that if we constantly tell ourselves that safety is our first priority, it paradoxically leads to complacency. This was certainly the case for his TV crew, who over the years slowly started experiencing more and more injuries on the job.

I think what the crew was experiencing – and what you or I could experience if we overexert our safety muscles all the time – is safety burnout. When you spend so much energy on any one area, even safety, it becomes mundane and eventually you just stop caring as much as you need to.

In saying "Safety Third", Mike Rowe is essentially saying that we have higher priorities that drive us to practice safety. These driving forces are our values, vision, and the mission we've set for ourselves. In a workplace, maybe that's serving the customers and making the money that pays the bills. In our personal life, maybe we're making friends and having new experiences. In both settings, those things "come before" safety.

So now maybe you're confused. The first several paragraphs of this chapter were all about putting safety first, and now we've spent the last few paragraphs talking about "safety third." So where exactly does safety belong, anyway?

Here's the bottom line: you have to live your life. Life is full of risks. Sometimes we risk a lot when we take a new job, or date a new person, or try a new skill. Yes, safety is incredibly important, and we should practice it wherever we go. At the same time, we have to go someplace before we can practice safety there.

Safety should always be a top consideration, but that doesn't mean it should be the only hand on the steering wheel of your life. I don't want to dissuade anyone from activities like starting their own business or going mountain climbing or bungee jumping simply because they are generally unsafe. You can still have your adventures, but bake safety into them so that you mitigate as much risk as possible.

So go out there and live your life. Don't get so focused on safety that you never take another risk. On the contrary, take those risks. Dare mighty things. Live life to the fullest. And when you do, take safety with you as your first step in being STRONG.

Safety in several settings

When we talk about safety as part of STRONG, we can break it up into three different settings: occupational safety, personal safety, and technological safety.

In the next few sections, we will dive into these areas, learning how to be safety-minded in each of them. Although we're dividing safety up into three different settings, there will always be overlap. Safety skills for your personal life absolutely impact your occupational life. Safety skills for technology could apply anywhere. Be mindful of these overlaps as you read.

Occupational safety

On average, Americans spend nearly a third of their lives at work. Due to this, occupational safety is incredibly important. According to the CDC, in 2019, 2.4 million people sustained injuries at work that were severe enough to need treatment in a hospital emergency room. That's a huge number! The CDC estimates that 1 in 64 workers are injured on the job every year. With statistics like this, it should be obvious why being safe on the job is so critical.

So how can we think safely in our occupation? We start by asking ourselves important questions about the work we're doing. By asking these questions, we give ourselves an opportunity to consider our environment and come up with safer ways to go about our work.

The first question to ask ourselves is, "Do I see any safety risks in my environment?" That seems like an overly obvious question to ask, but believe it or not, it can make a big difference for your safety in the workplace.

In numerous OSHA surveys conducted after a workplace injury, workers reported that they hadn't noticed whatever it was that caused the injury. These workers were not aware of their surroundings, and as a result, people were injured or even died on the job.

A safe environment looks different for every job, so as an employee you need to understand what changes can or cannot be made in your workplace to increase safety. Sometimes a safety risk can be removed from your environment, but other times, a safety risk cannot be eliminated, so you have to consider what steps to take when you're exposed to it.

This brings us to the next question to ask ourselves in the workplace: "Could I do what I'm doing more safely?" Sometimes, we find ourselves in an environment with safety risks that cannot be removed. Or maybe the environment doesn't have any major safety risks, but we need to perform duties that could be potentially unsafe.

When you find yourself in a potentially unsafe situation, ask whether you can adjust your actions to make the situation safer. Once again, this seems like common sense, but many workplace accidents are due to workers not using safe practices in their workplace. Whether it's standing on a swivel chair to reach something high or crossing an I beam at a construction site without a safety harness, there are often better ways to perform a task.

In the United States, employers typically cannot fire or penalize an employee for pointing out safety risks and refusing to perform a task until adequate safety measures are in place. This means that if you're asked to perform a task and you don't have the resources to do so in a safe manner, you can and should say so. Most employers will appreciate your safety-mindedness because in the long term, thinking safe will save them money and resources.

Having said that, this doesn't mean that an employee can simply refuse to complete a task because there are inherent risks involved. Some tasks are just naturally going to be more risky than others. If the employer makes every reasonable effort to make the task as safe as realistically possible, they've fulfilled their responsibility.

By now you've asked those two questions about safety, but there's still one more question to ask yourself: "Am I properly communicating safety risks?"

This can be the make-or-break point on safety. If you see a safety risk, and you have considered a more safe way to go about your task, but you haven't properly communicated that risk, the hazard hasn't really been eliminated.

Answering this question really requires a lot of critical thinking, not because communicating is hard, but because sometimes knowing the right person to contact and the right way to communicate those risks can be.

One of the biggest considerations in communicating safety risks is knowing with whom you need to communicate a safety concern. In some situations, it might be as easy as mentioning it to a coworker. For example, if your colleague ran an extension cord across a walking path, you could probably address the situation directly with that person.

On the other hand, in many cases it's important to make your supervisor aware of safety risks. Start by speaking politely about the situation. Offer to do what you can to improve the safety risk. This shows that you're invested in finding solutions. If the scenario with the cord going across the walkway took place because there were no outlets on the other side of the walking path, it would be worth asking your employer for an outlet installed on the other side of the walking path or suggesting some other solution to minimize the risk.

Once you've decided who to talk to about the safety concern, it's important to know how to approach them. Most of the time, people don't realize that they've created a hazard. It's important when you communicate your safety concerns that you don't start out in an angry or accusatory tone. Starting with a friendly suggestion or question is almost always the best way to open a dialogue. Then make a polite yet firm request. We'll talk more about being cordial with others in our next chapter, Teamwork.

By now you understand who to talk to and the best way to approach the situation. The final step is to follow up. If the safety concern was not remedied, take your concerns back to the person responsible or speak to their supervisor. Alternatively, if the safety concern was addressed, thank them for listening.

To recap, here are three questions you can ask yourself to have a safer workplace:

• Do I see any safety risks in my environment?
• Could I do what I'm doing more safely?
• Am I properly communicating safety risks?

Safety is everyone's responsibility in the workplace. If you're asking these questions, you're on track to start being a safety-minded worker.

Personal safety

The next area where safety is important is your personal life. Even though STRONG pertains primarily to the workplace, your personal life is an important part of who you are. STRONG is ultimately about making you a success, and leading a safe personal life will help you lead a more successful life both inside and outside the workplace.

Leading a safe life doesn't mean leading a life without fun. On the contrary, if you're the sort of person who lives for trips to new places, adventures like skydiving or bungee jumping, or even just a good amusement park, you don't have to stop. It simply means that even in the adventures that you go on, do them with safety in mind.

Again, there are three questions you can ask yourself in just about every setting that will help you lead a safe personal life.

The first question is, "Am I in a safe place?" A safe place doesn't necessarily mean a place completely devoid of risk. It means that you're in an environment that you can trust.

Take a minute to really think about the places you go regularly. How safe are they? What risks might be there that you've never considered before? Being able to answer these questions can help you make better decisions like when to go, how long to stay, who to go with, and how to spend your time there.

Sometimes you'll find yourself in an environment that has dangers. It's important to be able to identify what those dangers are. Ultimately, being able to identify the risks in your environment will make you more aware of your surroundings, and more likely to stay safe.

Another important question to ask yourself is, "Am I in a safe situation?" Again, I'm not suggesting that if you answer no, you necessarily hightail it out of there. It's a call to think about your situation.

A number of variables that can impact the safety of a situation. Sometimes the people you're with might pose a hazard to your safety. In other times, the activity itself might have safety risks. Think about all the elements of the situation that you're in and break them down into their individual components. Then look for areas where safety can be at risk.

Finally, one more question you can ask yourself is, "Have I established safe personal boundaries?" Setting boundaries for yourself helps you define who you are and helps you say yes or no.

Setting personal boundaries is like setting rules for your life. These rules are custom-tailored to who you are. For example, someone who struggles with addiction might set a personal boundary to avoid alcohol, while someone without these tendencies might not. Knowing who you are is an important part of knowing the boundaries you should set.

When we talk about setting boundaries, it's easy to only think about the things we choose not to do, but in reality, we also have to think about the things we will do. Along with setting a personal boundary, plan an exit route to help you maintain that boundary.

In part 1 of this book, we talked about having a mission, and I encouraged you to write out a mission statement. I would encourage you just as strongly to also write out a list of personal boundaries. By doing so, you solidify them and make them easier to live by.

To recap, these are three questions you can ask yourself to improve your personal safety:

• Am I in a safe place?
• Am I in a safe situation?
• Have I established safe personal boundaries?

Keeping yourself safe is an important part of being successful. By thinking about the settings you find yourself in, you'll be vastly better equipped for whatever challenges come your way.

Technological safety

In this modern age, technology is everywhere. Even the humble key fob for your car has more memory onboard than the Apollo spacecraft did! Many people have a smartphone, and Internet access is available just about anyplace you go.

With technology all around us, we must practice technological safety. Our identities, bank accounts, and even our personal lives have moved online. Scammers, phishers, and hackers are out there, and will gladly take everything you've got if you let them.

As with the other aspects of safety, there are questions we can ask ourselves to determine if we're practicing technological safety.

We should ask ourselves the first question every single time we go online: "How much should I be sharing?"

Today, the internet seems to be engineered to get us to put as much of our lives out there as possible. Social media makes it tempting to share all. Online influencers seem to put their entire lives online and encourage us to do the same. In this culture of liking and tweeting and reposting, it's easy to go too far and inadvertently put ourselves in unsafe situations.

Perhaps the most significant problem of oversharing is that once something is online, it's hard – if not impossible – to remove it. Sure, you can delete your post or photo, but there's no telling how many others made their own copies of what you shared before that happened. Even in apps that "guarantee" your information will not be saved, people have figured out ways to work around those safeguards.

How do you protect yourself from oversharing? When you get online, mindfully consider the necessity of what you want to share. Bernard Meltzer, the late radio host, is quoted as saying, "Before you speak ask yourself if what you are going to say is true, is kind, is necessary, is helpful. If the answer is no, maybe what you are about to say should be left unsaid." This is wise advice that can help you make good decisions.

The next question to ask yourself about technological safety is, "Do I see any red flags?" When you're dealing with others online, keep your eyes open. Often, if something doesn't seem right, it probably isn't.

One common area of online risk is dating. According to eHarmony, 40% of singles are using online dating. This is a huge number of people all looking for love, making them a ripe target for scammers. In 2021 alone, Americans lost $547 million to online romance scammers.

Another growing area of concern is technical support scams. These scams are operated from overseas call centers that pose as legitimate technical support. While they frequently prey on the elderly, they have also scammed many young people who didn't know better. In 2021, Americans lost $347 million to these scams.

These two types of fraud are only the tip of a very large iceberg. In 2021 alone, people lost a total of $5.8 billion to fraud in the United States. In nearly every instance of online fraud, the victims realize later on that there were multiple red flags they shouldn't have ignored.

Keep your eyes peeled for things like questionable email addresses, senders who claim to be popular or high-ranking officials, claims that sound too good to be true, and any other things that look like potential red flags to you. If you have any suspicion that any sort of online interaction isn't completely safe, do a lot of research – or simply walk away.

Finally, there is one more question we can ask ourselves to help practice better technological safety: "Am I keeping things secure?"

What does it mean to keep things secure, anyway? One big part of technological safety is password protection. Another is limiting use of things like credit card numbers or social security numbers. Finally, keep tabs on security over time.

Much of the online world requires password protection. Your email, social media accounts, and nearly every website you utilize want you to create usernames and passwords for access. Set strong passwords for these accounts. When possible, use special characters (such as spaces, punctuation, and symbols). Use long strings of words that only you know. Ideally, never use the same password across multiple sites. Finally, change your passwords from time to time so that if they do become compromised, your accounts will be more safe.

Also be careful when you share personal identifying information or financial numbers online. So many websites will ask for a card number and give you the option to save it on file. While this is convenient, especially at sites where you use your card a lot, it poses a security risk if that site is ever hacked. If you don't think you'll use a site frequently, don't save your data there.

Data breaches happen. Even if you've done everything to stay safe online, the websites you use are targets of hackers. There's a whole online world commonly called the dark web, where people sell data like passwords, credit card numbers, and identity information. From time to time, make a point of checking to see if your data is out there. There are numerous sites that can do this for you. One of the more popular sites is called 'have I been pwned?' at haveibeenpwned.com. On this site, you can check if your email address or phone number are showing up on any databases of stolen info. If they are, it's time to change passwords!

With the ideas in this section, you've made a good start into being technologically safe, but there is plenty more to learn about. Technology is also changing all the time, so keep up to date on recommended technological safety practices.

To recap, these are the three questions we asked ourselves:

• How much should I be sharing?
• Do I see any red flags?
• Am I keeping things secure?

Technological safety is important. By watching your steps with your technology, you're helping pave the way for a more successful life.

Putting it all together

Earlier in this chapter, we talked about how there will always be overlap among the three areas of safety we've looked into. Life isn't always neat and compartmentalized. We use technology in our personal and work lives. Who we are in our personal life impacts who we are at work, and vice versa. This is true for everything in life.

Take a moment to think about the safety measures currently in place in the various parts of your life. How effective are they? What areas can you improve? What steps can you make to improve your occupational, personal, and technological safety? Asking yourself these questions will help you to become a safer person, and ultimately a more successful person.

Chapter 6 –
Teamwork

The winning strategy

If one component of STRONG is most likely to determine your outcome in life, it is teamwork. How we function as part of a team not only reveals our character; it also directly results in our success. Andrew Carnegie called teamwork "the fuel that allows common people to attain uncommon results." More recently, entrepreneur Reid Hoffman said, "No matter how brilliant your mind or strategy, if you're playing a solo game, you'll always lose out to a team."

Before we go on, it's important to understand what teamwork means in the context of STRONG. One definition of teamwork is this:

> *"The process of working collaboratively with a group of people in order to achieve a goal."*

This just means that teamwork is people working together to accomplish something. These can be small goals or large, but to pull them off always requires one thing: your ability to work well with others.

In the context of the STRONG program, teamwork also relates to your role on the team. Often, teams consist of people with different specialties or abilities. Knowing what unique skills you bring to the table helps you become a more valuable part of your team.

You're always on a team

One secret to good teamwork is realizing that you are always part of a team, perhaps even multiple teams. Sometimes it's easy to identify your team, like when you're playing a sport or working on a group project. Other times it might not seem like you're on a team, like if you're the only person assigned to a project at work. Regardless, you are still on a team.

Many days, I work alone in my office. Am I still on a team there? Absolutely! Whether it's the board of directors, volunteers, or the people we support in the community, what I'm doing is part of a bigger picture that takes a lot of people to be successful.

It's also important to realize that you may be on multiple teams at once. You might have a work team, a team at home, a team of friends, and other teams of various shapes and sizes. You're probably even part of a few teams that you didn't even realize are teams. Can you think of any examples?

Teams are everywhere, and this is why practicing good teamwork is so essential to your success. This is true whether you're talking about success in your education, personal life, work, or family.

How to be a great teammate

If we know that teamwork is important and that teams are everywhere, where do we start in order to become better teammates?

The starting point for everything teamwork-related is personal conduct, or how you present yourself. Good personal conduct is essential to being a healthy part of a team. If you can't conduct yourself well, your whole team will struggle.

Interpersonal skills

Personal conduct is such an important part of teamwork that you can find it in nearly every ad for a job. Oftentimes, instead of listing "personal conduct" or "teamwork" on a job ad, hiring managers will refer to it as something else: "interpersonal skills." If you can develop these skills, you'll be a valuable asset to a team.

This raises a question: what are interpersonal skills? They include a whole slew of skills that all relate to how you work with others. When we talk about interpersonal skills in STRONG, we're specifically referring to a set of skills that make you a valuable teammate. These components include the following:

- Active listening
- Spoken communication
- Non-verbal communication
- Written communication
- Emotional intelligence
- Empathy
- Acceptance
- Conflict resolution
- Problem solving
- Customer service

Let's work through this list of crucial skills.

Active listening

The first part of being a good teammate is practicing good active listening. Active listening is, in short, being attentive to those around you. Unlike passive listening, which doesn't require any feedback on your part, active listening requires you to engage with the person talking.

Practicing active listening shows the other person that you're invested in the situation and value their time. Even if they don't say it out loud, people will generally respond better to an active listener than a passive listener.

So how can you be a good active listener? The first step is to look at the person to whom you're listening. This might seem fundamental, but it makes a big difference. If you look at a person, they know that you're focusing on them. This helps them feel comfortable working with you.

In many cases, just looking at the person isn't enough. You also need to remove distractions. Distractions come in many forms. Maybe it's putting the cell phone into your pocket, taking out earphones, shutting off a machine you're operating, or swiveling your chair to face away from the computer screen. Maybe it's excusing yourself for a moment from a conversation with someone else. No matter what it is, make sure that you're eliminating distractions so the person you're working with understands that they're your priority in that moment.

Once you're looking at the person and have removed distractions, the next step is to show them that you're listening. You can do this in multiple ways. Sometimes a small nod is all it takes to convey that you're following them. Other times, you can respond with an affirming statement like "okay."

Another great way to be an active listener is to rephrase and repeat what the person you're listening to has said. Start with a phrase like "what I hear you saying is" and finish with what they've said. Do this sparingly, but at times it may be beneficial, such as when someone is explaining something complex or giving directions. Being able to rephrase and repeat shows them that you're still with them.

Replying and giving feedback are also great ways to listen actively. Again, do this sparingly, as thinking of what you're going to say can be as big of a distraction as any cell phone. Before you reply, think about how your comments will reflect upon you as well as the rest of the team. When you give feedback, be sure to give feedback on the person's ideas and avoid making judgmental statements about the person themselves.

Spoken communication

Good spoken communication allows us to communicate our thoughts and ideas with one another more clearly and effectively.

Be sure that you speak clearly when talking to others. Don't mumble or run your words together. It's generally okay to speak with whatever natural accent you may have, but try to avoid slang or terms that your listener might not understand.

Nonverbal communication

Practice good body language while you're talking: stand or sit up straight and look at the person to whom you're talking. Many of the best communicators practice their nonverbal communication in front of a mirror or with a camera to hone their skills. This can be a valuable way to grow this skill if it gives you trouble.

Pay attention to your tone of voice, especially if you're communicating by phone or in a situation where you can't be seen.

Written communication

We live in a highly technological age where written communication is everywhere. Nearly every company uses writing to communicate both internally and with the public, whether that's emails, live messaging, or social media. Because of this, you'll make yourself a much more valuable team member if you have good written communication skills.

Here are a few helpful strategies to make you a good written communicator:

Avoid using shorthand, including texting slang, in business communications. Even commonly used shorthand like "lol" is unprofessional and unnecessary in professional communication. Some professions have professional shorthand such as what nurses use every day in their charting. This form of professional shorthand is acceptable in these jobs.

Whenever possible, use complete sentences. Try reading your written communication out loud to make sure it sounds correct. By doing this, you help ensure that your recipients will be able to understand what you're writing.

After you've finished writing something, go back through and edit. Keep things concise, and avoid run-on sentences. Having others review your work when possible is also a great resource to help make your writing more effective and well-written.

Emotional Intelligence

Put simply, emotional intelligence is the ability to be smart with your emotions. It can be easy to overlook, but how you react emotionally can significantly affect how well you get along with others. The following are a few ideas to help you hone your emotional intelligence.

Be aware of your emotions and practice self-regulation. Self-monitor your behaviors and be introspective of who you are. We'll cover introspection more in chapter 10.

Avoid going directly to strong emotional reactions like anger. It can be easy to get angry when things don't go your way. Instead of bursting out in rage or making a passive-aggressive comment, look for positive ways to release your anger, or better still, use your feelings to push you to improve the situation.

Practice positivity. Be a can-do person rather than an it-can't-work person. If you know for a fact something will not work, diplomatically suggest modifications that will make it work. Look for ways to motivate others. By practicing positivity, you raise morale and improve the environment for everyone.

Empathy

Learning to have empathy for others may be the best thing you can do to become emotionally intelligent. Being empathetic means that you consider the feelings and situations of others. When you listen to others, try to put yourself in their shoes. Don't rush to judge, but work to understand where they're coming from with their views.

Acceptance

Learning to accept others is a cornerstone of good interpersonal skills. Let's face it – you're going to run into a lot of different people in your life. Many will have beliefs, personalities, and ideas that are vastly different from your own. We have to bring ourselves to a place where we can see our teammates as respected and valued members of our team, even if they are different from us or we disagree. Being able to accept others will take you far in the workplace and beyond.

Conflict resolution

The last thing most managers want to do is spend their days acting as referee between employees. Being able to resolve conflicts with others will make you a valuable member of any team.

How do you resolve conflicts? Active listening is a great place to start. Hear out what the other person has to say. Be willing to own your mistakes and offer heartfelt apologies for them. Practice empathy and be willing to see the conflict from their point of view.

Avoid blaming or labeling people, and other tactics that deflect from facing your conflict. Instead, talk directly about the situation that's causing the disagreement. In some circumstances it can be helpful to table a conflict briefly until emotions have had a chance to cool down, as long as you do come back to address the issues. If needed, consider negotiating so that both parties can get some of what they want.

Problem-solving

Throughout this book, we've talked about the importance of being a problem-solver. This skill will come up again and again in life.

Knowing how to solve problems defines a leader and is a skill that nearly every employer wants.

One great tool for solving problems is the SODAS method. SODAS is an acronym for Situation, Options, Disadvantages, Advantages, and Solution. The way this works is that when you encounter a problem, you break it down into small steps, and work your way to a solution:

Situation: First, start by determining what situation needs to be solved.

Options: From there, brainstorm to come up with multiple options to address the situation.

Disadvantages: For each option, determine the most likely disadvantages for each.

Advantages: Now list the most likely advantages for each option.

Solution: Finally, pick the best option as your solution and put it into action.

Using a problem-solving strategy like SODAS is a great way to begin building your problem-solving muscles. Over time, you'll find that you can solve problems more naturally. Like all skills, problem-solving takes time to develop, so practice problem-solving whenever you can.

Customer service skills

Another attribute hiring managers are looking for is customer service skills. Sooner or later, most people in a company will interact with a customer, even if you typically work behind the scenes.

The interesting thing about learning customer service skills is that they're really a lot like the rest of the interpersonal skills listed above, except that they apply to a customer instead of a co-worker or supervisor. Because they are so similar to interpersonal skills, you've already learned many of them. Active listening, verbal communication, written communication, emotional intelligence, acceptance, conflict resolution, and problem solving are all part of having good customer service skills.

In addition to the skills above, it's also important that you give an extra degree of attentiveness to customers. Remember, in any business it is the customers, clients, patients, or patrons who bring in the funding to keep things going. To be a great teammate, do your best to go above and beyond for your customers.

For example, if a customer comes to you with a problem, never leave them with "I don't know" for an answer. Use your problem-solving skills to figure out a way to help them solve the problem. Alternatively, sometimes the solution to a problem is to help them find the person who can solve their problem. You can answer, "I don't know, but I'll gladly help connect you with a staff member who can help."

Customers want to feel valued and appreciated. So, good customer service means sincerely valuing and appreciating each customer. A positive facial expression, saying "thank you" to your customers, and letting them know you appreciate their patronage always goes a long way.

Initiative

Often, the difference between success and failure comes down to whether or not someone took initiative to act on what they saw. Being a person who jumps up, takes action, and does what needs to be done makes you an excellent teammate.

Sometimes we're tempted to say, "someone else can do that," or even "that's not my job." What would happen, though, if you took the initiative and chose to make it your responsibility? More than likely, the work will get done sooner, you'll feel good about your accomplishment, and others will recognize you as a team player.

We'll discuss taking initiative more in chapter 9.

Other important aspects of being a good teammate

The list of interpersonal skills we just covered is really just a starting point. We will cover some other interpersonal skills later on, such as accepting feedback and being a leader, in chapter 10.

Ultimately, the best advice is the Golden Rule. Be excellent to each other. Treat people with the same kindness and respect that you'd like to be treated with, and you'll be well on your way to being a great teammate.

Chapter 7 –
Reliability

Be there when you're needed

Prior to developing the STRONG program, I reached out to several employers in the community and asked what they were looking for in new hires. At the time, I was teaching skilled trades classes at a high school, and I had been looking for skills that my students would need to be successful. When I called these managers I expected them to tell me specific hard skills that a young person would need, such as how to use various hand tools or how to read a measuring tape.

Manager after manager told me the same thing. They needed employees with soft skills. They could teach the hard skills easily, but soft skills were often a different story. The number one thing on almost every manager's list of requirements: "I need workers who will show up when they're supposed to."

Why did showing up on time always seem to be the first thing they had in mind? I gave that question a lot of thought. What I soon realized is that if a worker isn't reliable, the entire team suffers.

One manager talked about the trouble he had recently when he hired three men for a job. One of the men was consistently late day after day. Because the job required three workers, this meant that at the start of the day, the other two workers would sit around unable to start until the third person showed up. This not only cost the company money, it slowed down their productivity.

Defining reliability

What comes to mind when you hear the word reliability? Do you think of someone who shows up on time? Or someone you can count on? These are both great examples of what it means to be reliable. In fact, they're almost the definition of reliable, which is as follows:

"the quality of being trustworthy or of performing consistently well."

Whether you realize it or not, you want the things in your life to be reliable. Imagine if your car was unreliable. Being stuck on the side of the road is no fun. Or what if you had cell phone service that only worked intermittently? Imagine having an emergency and discovering you can't call for help. The list could go on forever.

Being reliable is a crucial component of your STRONG skills. Being reliable means being someone who others can count on, all the time. A person who shows up when they are supposed to, does what they've agreed to, and can be counted on to complete their assignments is a valuable asset. This person is far more likely to be successful.

Time management

The best place to start learning to be reliable is time management. Time management is another one of those desired skills you'll see on job listings. Finding staff who can manage their time is important to employers, and being someone with good time management skills will make you more successful.

One place to start with time management is setting up personal routines. Personal routines are simply activities that you do on a set schedule. For most people, an easy place to start setting up routines is their morning, and a solid morning routine often helps with your job. Set an alarm to get up at the same time every day. Make a list of things you need to do, like eating breakfast and brushing teeth. Then, work toward completing your list every day. When you do the same things in the same order around the same time almost every day, you fall into a rhythm that's smooth and nearly automatic.

For example, if it takes an hour to complete your morning routine, the drive to work is usually 10 minutes, and you need to be at work by 8:00, then you know that you should probably be waking up by around 6:30. (If you're a snooze button person, factor that in, and set your alarm accordingly.)

Planning for the unexpected

Hold on. Are you thinking to yourself that my math in that example doesn't work out? After all, if your morning routine takes an hour, and your morning commute takes 10 minutes, you could actually wake up at 6:50, not 6:30, and be at work on time. The problem with that idea, however, is that it leaves no room for the unexpected.

Even the best routine can run into to problems. Maybe you spill food on your shirt or can't find your wallet. Maybe your car won't start and you need to find a ride or you get stuck in traffic on the way. Whatever the case may be, sometimes life doesn't go as planned. Give yourself time to compensate for the unexpected. It's always better to be a little early than a little late.

Good time management helps everyone

Being on time to work and other commitments isn't just beneficial to you, but to everyone involved. What you do in your occupation almost always impacts others. Because of this, it's important to be at your starting location and ready to start working on time or early. If you want to socialize, grab a coffee, or anything else, be sure that you arrive early enough to do these things before your workday begins. This ensures that others won't be held up waiting while you start your day.

Scheduling

Scheduling is another helpful component of good time management. Scheduling can take a lot of forms, but ultimately it's simply planning what you intend to happen at certain times and dates. For example, if you know that you get paid on the 1st and 15th of every month, scheduling your bills to be paid after those dates will help you manage your bank balance.

An advantage to getting your life on a schedule is that you're equipping yourself to follow your company's schedule more effectively. Nearly every business runs on a schedule. It's incredibly important that you follow your part of the schedule: showing up and leaving when you're supposed to, sticking to deadlines, or collaborating with coworkers.

Living on a schedule also means you can communicate your own needs to your manager in a timely manner. You'll earn a lot more respect with your employer if you can ask a month in advance for time off than if you suddenly have to skip work tomorrow.

Scheduling doesn't need to be difficult. There are numerous free online calendars that you can use right from your phone. If a digital calendar isn't your thing, buy a paper calendar or make your own planner by writing dates out in a notebook. Look for an option that will work for you.

Prioritizing

An important skill to develop is the ability to prioritize. Prioritizing is simply putting things in order of their relevance. By prioritizing, you can take stress off your plate by not feeling like you have to do everything at once. It can also help you get things done in a logical order.

One simple way to practice prioritizing is to write out everything you have to do on a sheet of paper. Next, divide another sheet of paper into four sections: A, B, C, and D.

Once you've done this, go through your list and transfer anything that's a high priority into section "A". High priority items would be tasks that are very important and need to be completed very soon. These are your must-do's. Next, place into section "B" all the medium priority items. These would be tasks that are still important but maybe not as urgent. Third, put your low-stakes items into section "C". These are things that aren't that important, and may or may not be urgent. Finally, whatever is left goes into section "D", for optional or ultra-low priority tasks.

As you divide your tasks into priorities, be aware of your co-workers and their priorities as well. Your prioritization can impact their workflow. If something seems like a "C" priority to you, but a colleague cannot start their project until you complete this task, that may actually be an "A" priority.

After you've divided your tasks into these priority assignments, you can sort them again within each section based on which tasks you will complete first, second, third, and so on. From there, start tackling the tasks one at a time, and be sure to pause to reassess your list from time to time.

Multitasking

We can often make our lives easier by combining tasks. This is called multitasking, and saves time and effort. A good example of multitasking is how we clean up a table after we eat. You probably don't walk one fork to the sink, then go back to the table and bring one knife over, and so on until the work is done. More than likely, you stack up a bunch of dishes and silverware and carry them all over to the sink at the same time and can do it while holding a conversation. That's how multitasking works.

Look for ways you can multitask to save time. Maybe you can work on multiple projects at once, or organize projects so you only need to make one trip to the copier. Finding ways to save steps will make you better at what you do, and make you more successful in general.

Giving your best effort

If you agree to take on a task, put your whole heart into it. When you work on a task, giving it your best is a great way to show that you're reliable. When you put in minimal effort, it shows, and in some situations putting in little effort might even be worse than not trying at all.

Dr. Martin Luther King, Jr. said, "If a man is called to be a street sweeper, he should sweep streets even as Michelangelo painted, or Beethoven composed music or Shakespeare wrote poetry. He should sweep streets so well that all the hosts of heaven and earth will pause to say, 'Here lived a great street sweeper who did his job well.'" If you live with this mindset, you'll rank among the most reliable of your peers and earn respect, even in the most unglamorous of jobs.

Keeping your word

One of the best ways to be reliable is to stick to your word. If you've agreed to something, don't back out of it at the last minute or go back on what you have said. If you've made a promise, keep it. If you've made plans to do something, hold yourself to those plans. This may mean being more careful of what and how much you commit to in the first place.

Being a person of your word makes you reliable. When people can count on you to do as you said, they'll be able to trust you, giving you more freedom and opening doors for growth and success. This is especially true in your work, where you often are asked to complete certain objectives and work independently.

Understandably, sometimes emergencies or other situations come up that are outside of our control. While you should still stick to your word if possible, there may be times when you aren't able to do so. In that case, respect the other people involved by communicating the situation as soon as possible.

Communicate

If you want to become more reliable, you need to communicate. One of the biggest complaints I heard from hiring managers while developing the STRONG program was an overall lack of communication from employees. Poor communication can often be grounds for termination, especially if you repeatedly "no call, no show" at your job.

I cannot stress this enough – if you are going to miss work, you MUST reach out to your employer, speak to the correct person in charge of the day's scheduling, and let them know! If your job gives you a specific procedure for calling in, follow that procedure. I have never encountered a manager who thought it was acceptable for employees to just skip a day without calling in sick.

Additionally, you need to let your employer know about your absence as soon as reasonably possible. If you're sick on a Tuesday and you're scheduled to work on Wednesday, don't wait until just before your shift the following day. Call on Tuesday. If you plan to take a vacation in a few months, contact your scheduler as early as they'll accept it.

Of course, communication doesn't end at calling in on sick days or scheduling vacation time. If you want to be known for your reliability, learn to communicate all the time. Update your superiors on project statuses. When you have questions, take the initiative to ask. Having a strong, open line of communication with your supervisors will help you move forward in your career.

Project management

Managers and supervisors shouldn't be the only people who can manage a project. Having good project management skills makes you more valuable to your team. When your supervisor can trust you to take on a project, you'll be more likely to achieve success.

Managing a project begins with establishing a mission and goals for the project. (For a refresher on missions and goals, look back at chapter 1.) Next, determine the resources that you need for your project. This could be people, materials, locations, or time. Then lay out a schedule that breaks the project down into small, manageable steps. Identify priorities, just as we discussed above, so that you focus on the most important components. Along the way, be sure to track your progress and communicate it as necessary.

Working independently

Being able to work independently is a skill that can take you a long way. While you are always part of a team, there will be times where you will be expected to work on your own. The ability to not only work apart from coworkers, but without constant supervision, is a highly sought-after skill.

Working independently starts with self-awareness: being aware of your performance and being able to monitor and correct yourself. This requires you to take time to ask yourself how you're doing and then to be objective in how you answer.

Being aware of what needs to be done is also important to working independently. If a supervisor assigns you to a task, they don't want you to come back again and again asking, "What's next?" We'll cover this topic in detail in chapter 9 about noticing.

You should also be able to self-motivate. Don't depend on a supervisor or coworkers to keep you going. If a task becomes challenging, press on and get the work done anyway without giving up. Developing the ability to do this can take a lot of work at first, but the good news is that the more you do it, the easier it gets.

Finally, become someone who owns your mistakes and weaknesses. If you refuse to admit your mistakes, or worse still, you blame your mistakes on others, then any project you're working independently on is at risk of falling apart. We'll discuss this topic more in chapter 10.

Finishing what you started

When you take on a task, see it through to the end. If you start something and say it will get done, it's ultimately your responsibility to make sure it happens.

It can be easy to abandon a project, especially when it gets difficult, but it's important to carry on and finish what you have committed to. Even when your circumstances change and completing a task is no longer possible, you still shouldn't abandon the task – find someone else to take it over or otherwise make sure it is still completed.

Becoming a leader

Something I've hinted at through the book so far but haven't stopped to spell out is that if you become STRONG, you will become a leader. The tools you're learning about in this book are the tools of good workers, but they're also the tools of leaders. Remember, the whole point of this book is to equip you for success. Becoming successful often involves becoming a leader.

We'll discuss leadership in more detail in chapter 10, but I am wrapping up this chapter with it because, frankly, it's important for you to start building a leadership mindset, and being reliable is a great place to start. Maybe you're a student. Maybe you're a janitor. Maybe you're a shift manager. Regardless of your current role, becoming a reliable person helps you become a better leader. Becoming a better leader opens doors for future opportunities. Those future opportunities are what lead to your success.

Practice reliability. Learn to live it. Become a person who is driven to be the most reliable person in the room, and you'll not only be STRONG, you'll become a leader.

Chapter 8 –
Orderliness

Beautiful chaos

I'll make a confession: this is a challenging chapter for me. And I don't mean a challenging chapter to write; it's challenging for me to live. Like millions of others, I have been diagnosed with ADHD. One aspect of this condition is that my mind sometimes works in a way that's almost the opposite of orderly. My thoughts come out cluttered and disorganized, and the world I create around me starts to look that way as well. If there's one aspect of STRONG that I personally have to fight to do well in, it's orderliness.

Now I want to be clear – ADHD is a legitimate disability and does make being orderly challenging. Beside ADHD there are other situations that can also make being orderly difficult. All the same, with the right strategies in place, these conditions can be managed.

Sometimes, I live in a state of what I call "beautiful chaos." As I write this, I'm scanning my desk. Here are a few of the things that stand out. Seven sticky notes of information scattered about. Parts from a current project near my monitor. A miniature robot. A bottle of wood glue. A plastic shopping bag.

All of these items sound random, and to some extent, they are. However, they all have purpose. The wood glue is a reminder that there's a woodworking project I'm working on. The sticky notes have information on various "A" and "B" priorities. The robot is a reminder to put together more curriculum for the robotics class I teach. The shopping bag is a reminder to fill out a rebate form for that store. So while my desk does have the appearance of chaos , all of these things have meaning, and more importantly, they all help me live an orderly life in a way that works for me.

Like me, you may need to find ways to make the STRONG program work for you. Don't skip any part of the program, but it's okay if you tailor it to who you are. You're a unique individual, and STRONG can fit you, even if there are areas that are more challenging.

Of course, there are limits to this. My desk, which sits in my personal office, can be organized in such a way that it works for me. However, I need to keep in mind that outside my office, the rest of this space is for everyone. I need to practice more conventional orderliness there, so that my own "beautiful chaos" doesn't become someone else's disaster area.

Additionally, no matter who you are or how you operate, some things will just make life easier. If you have a bunch of wrenches, it's always going to be easier to have them sorted than laying in a pile. Sorting things and putting them in order is a good practice, even if you do sort things using your own methodology. This is just a fact of life.

I get by with a little help from my friends

This brings me to another important aspect of being successful: friends and family. When I'm struggling with elements of STRONG due to my own shortcomings, I often look to those closest to me to help me do better. At our organization, I rely on my wife and volunteers to help me organize things that, with my ADHD, if I tried to do them myself I'd get lost. Their help keeps me in check and helps me be orderly.

Self-awareness is a big part of being STRONG. You have to understand your strengths and weaknesses, and you have to find ways to compensate for them. Getting started in an area that you struggle with can be hard, and that's okay. Find mentors who can help. If there's an area you excel in, step up and mentor someone else.

What is orderliness?

Before we discuss how to be orderly, let's look at what it means and why it's important. In the dictionary, a couple definitions of orderly stand out:

1. Given to keeping things neat or well-arranged.

or

2. Adhering or conforming to a method or system.

Both of these definitions are true in the workplace, and both are part of leading an orderly life. Keeping things neat and arranged helps you be more efficient on the job, as does sticking to methods and systems. This is so important that the Houston Chronicle wrote that orderliness was "one of the most important transferable job skills a worker can possess."

When I spoke to hiring managers while developing STRONG, orderliness came up over and over. In the office setting, workers failing to organize data or paperwork leads to missed payments and billing errors that cost the company money. In skilled trades, crews who don't keep their tools and supplies organized lose time searching for what they need or going out to purchase something they already have, and create safety hazards when things are left laying out. Wherever you turn, orderliness is in demand.

Sorting

Sorting is a great place to start learning about orderliness. We sort everything from thoughts to clothes to data on a spreadsheet. In a workplace, you may receive documents to sort, or you may have to sort physical items, such as tools and parts. In any case, being able to sort is a necessary component of being successful.

Let it go

The first step of sorting is purging. Go through what you're sorting and look for the items you don't need. If this is difficult, consider setting up some sort of method or system to help you determine what to keep and what to purge. For example, I have a friend who once per year goes into their closet and turns all their clothes hangers around so they're backwards. When they wear clothes they put the hangers back the right way. At the end of the year when they go to do it again, they discard or donate the clothes on hangers that are still backwards.

Of course, you may not have a year to decide what to purge. When you need to make a quick decision, consider bringing in an outside person who doesn't have an emotional attachment to what you're sorting. Since when you sort something you care about, it can be easy to get attached and hold onto things you don't need, bringing in someone more objective can help you identify which items aren't necessary.

As you purge items, consider their future. If you're purging papers, do they contain sensitive information that should be shredded? If you're purging physical items, are they worn out and ready to be thrown out, or will you sell or donate them? Sorting your purged items will help you make sure that everything lands where it belongs. If you can't decide right away whether to purge or keep something, start a "maybe" pile and come back to those items later.

Long-term storage

As you consider what you will and won't purge, think about how frequently you use an item. Sometimes there are things that we want to keep because we will use them again, but at the same time we don't use them very often. In these cases, long-term storage may be an option.

When you're deciding whether to put something into long-term storage, consider the item's frequency of use, its scarcity, and overall value. Frankly, in some cases it may be better to get rid of the item and buy or rent one when the need arises. If it's easy to purchase or rent, and you don't know when you'll need it again, you may decide to let go of it for now and plan to pick up another one if and when you need it.

Alternatively, if an item is hard to come by, or if you know when you'll use the item again, then it's a good candidate for long-term storage. For example, you may know you'll use Christmas decorations every December. Remember, the space to store items costs money, so cut down on long-term storage space when possible.

A place for everything

Once you've finished purging, the next step is to make space to store the items you're keeping. When you have room for everything that you're getting ready to sort, it will be orderly once it's sorted. Whatever the medium may be, whether it's shelving, boxes, hangers, folders, gigabytes, etc., be sure to have more available space than you need. So for example, if you have 10 wrenches, make space for 12.

There are at least two reasons to have extra space. First, it will give you room to move things around and try different organization styles. Second, this allows space to expand into if you acquire more items later. You may not need the space today, but you could someday, and it's best to be prepared. There isn't a one-size-fits-all suggestion for how much extra space you might need, but an extra 10-20% is a good place to start, and you can adjust that to fit what you're sorting. You don't want excessive amounts of unused space as this becomes wasteful, but you do need room to grow.

Everything in its place

Once you've ensured that you have adequate space, it's time to start sorting. Sorting can be a daunting task. Sometimes there are multiple ways to sort things. Consider this list of ten very different items:

- Giraffe
- Shoe
- Skyscraper
- Pizza
- Screwdriver
- Monkey
- Pencil box
- 3D printer
- Car
- Mouse

How would you organize this? We could organize the list by size, from mouse up to skyscraper. We could sort it into categories of living and nonliving items. We could alphabetize it. There are probably a dozen more ways this list could be organized and all of them are valid. So when you have multiple ways to organize something, which one do you choose?

In a workplace, start by looking at how existing items are organized or ask management if there is a practice in place already for sorting. Sometimes though, there won't be an established method of sorting. In these situations, it will be up to you to decide the most helpful way to sort things. Think about how you and others use the items, and find a way to sort them that makes practical sense.

Sort often

Once you've sorted items, you'll also need to work to keep them sorted. We talked in chapter 7 about building routines. An important routine you can develop is to regularly go through your things to sort them. Always keeping things sorted ensures that when you need something it's there for you.

As with determining how much additional space you need, there's no rule set in stone for how often you should re-sort items. You don't want to waste time and sort constantly when it's not needed. At the same time, by sorting more often you ensure that things don't get out of control. For the sake of building good habits, sorting items you use frequently every day and items you use less frequently every week is a good starting point. You can adjust from there.

Daily orderliness

Sorting and clearing out clutter is only a small part of orderliness. In addition, we can be orderly in our day-to-day tasks. By making plans, looking at what needs to be done, and following through in an orderly manner, you'll accomplish more in the same time.

Planning ahead

Get an orderly start by planning out a project before you begin. When you plan to do something, whether it's a project at the job site, a craft, or even a written work, it's crucial to know what you need before you begin. Start by considering all the tools, materials, and information you need, and build a supply list.

Once you've made your supply list, go through and make sure you have each thing you need. If some things on the list might be difficult to come by, try to gather those items first, so that if you run into snags in acquiring them you won't have to scrap the entire project. While you're stockpiling items before you start, it can be helpful to have someplace to store them so they don't get lost.

Focusing

Being able to focus on whatever task you're working on not only ensures that you'll spend more time paying attention to details, it also means that you'll get done more quickly. To help you focus, eliminate distractions and break your project into small, easily accomplished segments. Take breaks along the way to help you keep from losing focus or patience.

Picking up

When you're finished with a project, clean up everything involved with it right away. Return tools to where they belong. Put back furniture or supplies. Reset your space to the way it was before you began. Doing this helps you prepare for the next project that will come your way.

Maintenance

Whether it's an office or a construction site, maintaining your workspace matters, and it is everyone's responsibility. Even if you work where there are dedicated housekeeping or maintenance staff, everyone still has to do their part to keep the workspace in optimal condition.

As you go about your day, be on the lookout for things that are out of place and return them to where they belong. If you spot clutter, take a moment to declutter the space. If you find a drawer that needs sorting and you have the time, go ahead and sort it. These habits will help both you and your coworkers find things when you need them, which will help your workspace to be a place where you can work more effectively.

Keep in mind the old saying: "a stitch in time saves nine." In other words, by maintaining your space and keeping it in good condition, you save yourself bigger trouble down the road.

Orderliness ties into everything

Like each of the other components, orderliness shows up all throughout STRONG. Being orderly is a big part of practicing safety, as an orderly space is a safer space. Being orderly makes you a better teammate and more reliable. Orderliness plays roles in noticing and growing as well. If you practice the skill of being orderly, you'll make learning the rest of STRONG much smoother.

In the next chapter, we're going to talk about noticing what needs to be done. While much of the context of chapter 9 deals with noticing the work that needs to be done around you, it's also important to notice the things in your space that can be made orderly. Making your space more orderly will make your life simpler, and your work more efficient.

Orderliness isn't easy for all of us, but it can be done. Find the groove that works for you. Purge what you don't need. Sort the rest. Keep things sorted, and remember to look for ways to maintain your space. If you do this, you're on your way to becoming STRONG.

Chapter 9 –
Noticing

Notice *and* act

Have you ever found yourself "people watching?" If you're in a busy place like a shopping center, it can be fascinating to observe the people around you. The things they do, the people they talk to, it can tell a story even if you're not close enough to hear a word they say. What would you do, though, if you saw something distressing? Say, for example, you saw someone acting violently toward another person. Would you intervene or just keep watching?

In 1964, a woman named Kitty Genovese was stabbed to death outside her apartment in New York City. During the altercation that led to her stabbing, according to reports, at least a dozen of her neighbors were there, they all witnessed the crime, and none of them intervened.

Psychologists later coined this behavior the "bystander effect," a condition where people see a situation where they could make a difference but don't step in. Psychologists believe there are a couple reasons for this. First, there's a diffusion of responsibility: seeing that others are around makes people more willing to decide that it's not their problem. Second, there is a social influence factor: people don't act because nobody else is acting. Regardless of the cause, the bottom line is that just noticing isn't enough. To make a real difference, you have to act.

Take initiative

The exact same thing is true in the workplace. Sometimes it will be easy to see the next step or what we could do to make a situation better, but we don't do it. The result of this workplace bystander effect is that nothing improves, and often things get worse.

In STRONG, observing is only half of noticing. The other half is taking initiative. When we notice something, the follow-up to that is to act on it. We don't walk away or leave it for someone else. We take care of it. Taking initiative is inseparable from the noticing component of STRONG. You simply cannot have one without the other.

When you notice something in the workplace, the next step is to act on it appropriately. This doesn't mean charge in like a superhero. Some things you notice in the workplace can be solved simply; others require additional people's involvement. Regardless of how it should be settled, the important thing is that you act so it does get settled.

What to notice

Being observant not only helps you do your job; it can also lead to advancement and success in the workplace. So what is it we're supposed to notice, anyway? The short answer to that question is "everything."

But "everything" isn't a very useful answer, so let's break it down. There are seven areas where noticing can help in the workplace:

1. Notice the work that needs to be done
2. Notice the fine details
3. Notice things that can be improved
4. Notice opportunities for growth and advancement

5. Notice roadblocks to success
6. Notice others doing well
7. Notice others who need assistance

Let's explore these in greater detail.

Notice the work that needs to be done

Something that hiring managers often seek is initiative. We're going to discuss this more in chapter 10, but the conversation has to start with noticing. Many managers want workers who can identify the work around them that needs to be done – *before* being told. Be the sort of person who looks for work that needs to be completed, then take initiative to get the work done.

Notice the fine details

Employers want detail-oriented employees. Attention to detail means that you're more likely to catch mistakes while they're small. This prevents little problems from turning into big catastrophes. When you can pick out small details that need improvement, you're also making the work you do more credible.

Imagine reading a book about vocabulary and finding a misspelled word. Even though it's only a tiny mistake, it could lead to the reader losing trust in the entire book. Or imagine noticing that random screws are missing from the fuselage of an airplane. Passengers are going to think twice before boarding, not confident about what shape the engines are in. Focus on details, and you'll set yourself up for success.

Notice things that can be improved

It can be easy to spot things that need improvement. Maybe it's a safety procedure that could use revising, or a workplace activity that could be made better. When you notice these areas for improvement, step up and be the person that offers to make the change. Don't be a person who shrugs off this responsibility because it's "not my job," or because "somebody else can do it." If you see something that needs improvement and is within your ability to do, oftentimes there's nobody better to do it than you.

Notice opportunities for growth and advancement

Noticing opportunities for growth and advancement means that you're looking for ways to better yourself. This is so important! Bettering yourself is essential to becoming a success, so if you're not actively looking for ways to grow, you're missing out on chances to become more successful.

Many employers offer programs aimed at helping their employees grow, such as tuition assistance, management training programs, and sometimes even perks like gym memberships. Ask your employer or HR department what opportunities are available, and take advantage of them.

Notice roadblocks to success

Just as it's important to look for opportunities to grow, it's also important to be on the lookout for roadblocks to your success. Obstacles come in all shapes and sizes. For example, you may have coworkers who tend to steal attention or pass blame to others. Or perhaps there are limitations from advancing to higher positions in your current role. You have to be aware of roadblocks before you can successfully navigate around them.

Notice others doing well

There's a saying that "a rising tide lifts all boats," and it's definitely true when it comes to recognizing others doing well. By identifying others' strengths and areas that they are doing well in, you're creating allies that will lead to your own success. You're also creating an environment that others want to be in, making everyone happier and more productive.

Notice others who need assistance

Finally, keep your eyes open for those who need a hand. I can't stress enough how important it is to be ready to assist those around you. When you notice someone who needs assistance and then act on it, you're empowering that person to find their success, you're being a good teammate, and you're establishing yourself as someone who is reliable. It's a win for everyone involved.

Noticing leads to growth

In the next chapter, we're going to talk about growth, and a sure way to grow is through noticing. If you're the sort of person who can notice what needs to be done and take action to do it, then you're ready to grow and well on your way to success.

Chapter 10 –
Growing

Last but not least

While growing is the last component of the STRONG acronym, it is just as important. Being able to grow as a person is essential to your future success. When we allow ourselves to learn and grow, we ensure that we can adapt to whatever might come our way. In fact, every step of STRONG requires you to grow if you want to implement it effectively.

Employers are also looking for workers who can grow. An employee who won't accept feedback, correction, or training isn't much use to most managers. This attitude can lead to a range of negative consequences, including termination. Even if you come to a new job with every hard skill the job requires, it's still a new environment, and you need to be open to growing and learning how you can fit into that organization.

Growth is the pathway to advancement, promotion, and ultimately success. The accomplished people of this world are those who look for opportunities to grow and embrace chances to learn new things. If you want to get ahead, then be open to feedback, correction, and advice, especially from those who have gone before you.

Lance's story

When I was teaching high school welding classes I had a student we'll call Lance. He loved welding, and his dream was to become a welder when he left school. Lance was preparing to graduate in December of his senior year, and during his last month in my class he lined up a job with a welding company back in the small town where he grew up.

Before he left in December I spoke with Lance. I reiterated the STRONG program that I'd been teaching in school. I told him that if he wanted to be the best welder out there, he needed to go find the guys who'd been doing it for decades and learn everything he could from them. If he could do that, I told him, he'd eventually be the best there was.

Our school didn't have a graduation ceremony for December graduates, so Lance came back for the ceremony in May. I caught up with him before the ceremony started and asked how things had been going with his welding.

Lance informed me that he'd done what I had told him and actively looked for opportunities to learn from the older welders there. On top of that, he was constantly practicing and had even taken on welding projects for local farmers. As a result of his growth, he said he'd already been promoted multiple times within his company.

Curious, I asked him about his pay. He told me how much he was making, and I was a little concerned by it. It was a reasonable monthly salary for a new welder, but with the number of promotions he had talked about, I felt that he should be receiving more. I asked him if that was really all he was making per month.

"Oh no, Mr. Clements," he told me. "That's not how much I make in a month, that's my weekly pay." Needless to say, I was shocked. Thanks to practicing STRONG on the job, within five months Lance had advanced to the point where his weekly pay was comparable to a starting welder's monthly pay. Lance was earning far more every month than I was as his teacher!

While not every case will be as impressive as Lance's, he stands as a shining example of what can happen when you're willing to grow. Being willing to grow leads to success. On the other hand, refusing to grow can lead to your downfall. Let's take a look at a few popular examples.

Grow or die

It was January 2010, and everybody who was anybody had a Blackberry. It was dominating the market with a stunning 43% share of smartphone subscribers, according to the January 2010 Comscore report. Their nearest competitor, Apple, held a comparatively paltry 25% of the market. Research in Motion, the creators of Blackberry, were on top of the world.

There was a problem, though. Apple and Google had both begun selling smartphones with touchscreen interfaces. By all measures, this looked like the way of the future. But Blackberry had invested heavily in the full keyboards built into their phones. It was so ingrained into their brand that they refused to adopt full-phone touchscreens.

Fast forward to January 2022. Blackberry users made up less than 0.5% of the market share. Research in Motion was losing money hand over fist. They made a decision, and all Blackberry services were halted by the end of the month. In other words, they closed up shop.

Then there was Blockbuster Video. At their peak, they were the number one video entertainment business in America. They were in nearly every community coast-to-coast. If you wanted to rent a video, you'd "make it a Blockbuster night."

But then something changed. Little red kiosks started showing up all over the country. The RedBox era had officially begun. RedBox took a chunk out of Blockbuster's revenue, but the final blow was yet to be delivered.

Before long, another competitor, Netflix, stepped onto the scene. At first they offered DVDs by mail, but before long they started into another revolutionary idea: streaming movies directly online. The technology was new, and most people still rented videos, so Blockbuster made a call – they weren't going to adapt.

The result was catastrophic. In just a few years, Blockbuster went from number one to bankruptcy. Today, the company no longer exists, and the online streaming that they refused to adapt to has become the most popular way to watch movies.

The list of these companies could go on ad nauseam: Polaroid, Sears, K-Mart, Borders, ToysRUs, and even online companies like MySpace are all well-known examples of what happens when you refuse to adapt. If you're unwilling to grow, the end result is always the same: you die.

Learning to grow

Growth is clearly important. So how do we do it? What empowers us to become more than what we are now, able to do more with our lives than we have done before? There are some skills to learn that will help you become a person who grows.

Be a self-starter

If you want to succeed, learn to be a self-starter. All this means is that you don't rely on others to get you going. Whatever the case may be, whether it's getting up in the morning or starting your daily routine at the office, push yourself to get going without being told. Take initiative on projects that better you or your company. Give yourself pep talks or otherwise motivate yourself so that when an opportunity to grow arises, you seize it without needing to be asked.

Be self-motivated

Right along with being a self-starter is being self-motivated. Life gets hard. Things will stack against you. When times get tough, being self-motivated will get you through to better times.

Being self-motivated doesn't always mean you're cheery and peppy and in a good mood. Being self-motivated means that you have grit. It means when you come up against challenges, you push through them and keep moving forward. Being able to motivate yourself without others telling you to do so is a powerful tool for growth.

Introspection

Introspection is defined as:

"The examination or observation of one's own mental and emotional processes."

In other words, it's all about you being aware of who you are and what you're thinking and feeling. Being introspective is an important step to growing.

If you want to be an introspective person, the first step is to start paying attention to the things you do and the thoughts you have. The next step is to ask yourself why you have those thoughts and behaviors. This isn't meant to be a self-depreciating exercise, but rather a way for you to understand why you are the way you are.

Once you've started to consider the why, the next step is to consider how you can improve yourself. What skills are required in your occupation? What behaviors are more effective than others? What changes can you make to how you think and what you do to become more growth-oriented?

After you've done all of this, the final step is to put your changes into practice. Self-monitor your behaviors, and look for the those you want to change. When you catch yourself doing them, stop right away and take a better path.

A word of advice: don't expect changes to happen overnight. Some of the aspects of who you are have been instilled in you from an early age. Changes take time. Start with small steps you can take to change how you think or behave, reward yourself for following through, and keep taking small steps toward your success.

Problem-solving

Problem-solving has come up several times in this book, and for good reason – it's an important skill! Knowing how to solve problems is also an essential part of being able to grow.

Problem-solving isn't just an external behavior or a skill you use in the world around you. It's also something you can use to better yourself. Think of a change you want to make. Maybe in your introspection you discovered something that you'd like to do better. Use problem-solving to come up with plans. Ask what obstacles are in your way. Consider how you can handle those obstacles. Using problem-solving this way can be a great method to help you grow.

Critical thinking

Like problem-solving, critical thinking is a skill that goes a long way both in the world around you as well as internally as you become growth-oriented. Critical thinking is a process of considering your thoughts on a topic, especially if it involves conflicting information. When done well, it can help you see past your own biases and find the truth in a situation.

The first step to thinking critically is to identify the root issue. So often, what we think is the cause of a conflict is not. If you have conflicting thoughts or viewpoints, look for the commonalities in them, and see if you can determine what the root of the conflict actually is.

Once you've gone that far, the next step is to research the information given. Look for ALL the facts, not just facts that agree with your own beliefs. Sometimes it's even helpful to write out all the facts from the situation, so you can physically see them in front of you.

With all the facts collected, it's time to turn inward and challenge your biases. Ask yourself what flaws your assumptions might have. Look for places where what you assumed doesn't add up. This is an important step that many people miss, and it can make or break the critical thinking process.

The final step is to determine what the truth of the situation is. This step can be incredibly challenging because sometimes parts of what you believed going into the critical thinking process turn out to be wrong. When this happens, remember that this is a good thing. In fact, thinking critically is all about finding false thoughts you had and correcting them. Be proud of yourself when critical thinking leads to changing your thoughts. It means that you're growing!

Patience

Patience is one of the hardest skills to develop. If you tend to be an impatient person, learning to slow down and accept things as they come can be exceedingly frustrating. Still, patience is crucial for being able to grow. When we want to change ourselves or the world around us, we must acknowledge that this takes time, and that most things don't happen right away.

There are ways you can learn to be a more patient person. Try taking a deep breath when you get frustrated with how slow things are moving. Practice introspection when something is making you impatient, and ask yourself why you're struggling. Learn not to get wrapped up in "the small stuff." Once you find a technique that works for you, keep it in mind as your go-to in the moment when you're impatient.

Initiative

If you want to grow as a person, you need to take initiative. This means that when you find a situation that needs to be changed, you actively choose to step out and improve it.

In your workplace, others will notice you for taking initiative. Hiring managers value self-driven people, and people who take initiative often accomplish more than those who need constant direction. It will also develop you into a better person, especially as you learn to take initiative on steps to improve yourself.

To take initiative, start with identifying what needs to be changed for the better. Next, consider ways to make that change. Sometimes taking initiative can be as simple as communicating your ideas. Other times, you may need to be the one to carry out the changes. If that's the case, act on what you've identified to start making the improvements. Problem-solve as needed to address hurdles along the way.

Accepting feedback

To be a person who is able to grow, you need to accept feedback. Feedback is input or insight into what you're doing, especially what you can do differently to improve.

Feedback will come in many forms. It might be a friend mentioning something you said or did earlier. It may be a boss criticizing you on your work. Sometimes feedback is easy to accept, and other times it's exceedingly difficult. But we need to face the difficulty to truly grow.

When someone gives you feedback about anything, the best response in that moment is to say "okay," and thank the person for their feedback. Even if you don't agree with the feedback you're being given, being able to receive it and move on keeps the situation from escalating. You can ask questions to clarify, expand on what you know, or demonstrate that you are taking it seriously. Just be sure not to demand examples or use questions to defend your actions.

If you agree with the feedback, work to integrate it into your life. If you disagree, first use critical thinking to determine why you don't like it. Is what they said unfounded or do you dislike it because it was hard to hear? Are you taking it as a judgment on your identity rather than a statement about your actions? Are they speaking from values that don't align with your own? Difficult though it may be, if you don't like the feedback because it was hard to hear, yet you conclude that it is valid feedback, choose to implement it anyway.

Feedback is a gift. When someone gives you feedback, they're showing you that they value you enough to give you an opportunity to learn and grow.

Leadership

The next few sections of this chapter will discuss leadership. Leadership is an important part of growing as a person. To be a leader, you don't need to be a manager or director. By showing good leadership in your current position, you often open the door to moving up into bigger roles.

A leader, by definition, is someone who has authority or influence. By being someone who others can trust and look up to, takes initiative, and can see the big picture, you're acting as a leader, no matter what your official role is.

What makes a good leader? There are a number of skills that leaders possess. Many we have already discussed in this book: active listening, empathy, verbal and written communication, patience, time management, and problem solving. In addition, here are a few other important skills for leading well.

Authenticity

To be a leader, be authentic. This simply means be yourself. People won't follow the lead of someone who appears fake. Living an authentic life inside and outside the workplace establishes you as someone who others can follow.

Mentoring

Real leaders are interested in making more real leaders. If you want to be a leader, take interest in others. Forming mentoring relationships is a powerful way to help others grow and reach their full potential. As we learned in chapter 2, having a mentor is a key ingredient of being successful. Acting as a mentor contributes to your success as well.

Delegation

Delegation is letting go of a responsibility so that others can handle it. Some leaders try to hold onto everything themselves and micromanage their workers. This is unhealthy and leads to burnout. As a leader, you must believe that others around you can be leaders as well, then delegate tasks to those leaders. This will free you to do more.

Reading

Do you want to be a great leader? Read. Read trade journals for your work. Read news and magazine articles. Read novels. Reading is one of the best ways to boost your brain and help you expand your perspective. By being a reader, you create opportunities to encounter new thoughts and ideas. This helps you grow, and helps you lead.

Worth the effort

Growth is rarely easy. In fact, of the six areas of STRONG, growing can be one of the most challenging. Still, you owe it to yourself to put in the effort. Without growth, becoming more than you are is impossible. Again, implementing any of the other areas of STRONG is in itself an act of growing.

Being capable of growth enables you not only to make yourself better, but to make the environment around you better as well. It's worth the effort and in the end it will help you become STRONG.

Chapter 11 –
STRONG wherever you are

Take STRONG with you

Congratulations! You've made it through all six components of STRONG. Now, it's time to look ahead and put all the pieces together so you can be STRONG wherever you go. It may have been a lot to take in, but if you've taken your time and given serious thought to the words in the previous chapters, you've already started on a path toward success. And you can always refer to the chapters again anytime you need to.

Remember that simply reading this book cannot change your life. If you want the better chances for success, improved conditions at work, and opportunities for advancement that come from living out the STRONG program, you need to practice the lessons in this book every day.

In chapter 10, I introduced you to Lance. What made Lance successful was that he lived the STRONG program every day inside and outside of work. He practiced safety in his welding job and at home. He was an excellent teammate, on and off the clock. He was reliable, waking up hours before work so he could practice his craft and still arrive to work early. He was orderly, and kept his worksite and home shop clean. Wherever he was, he noticed what needed to be done and took the initiative to do it. Finally, he kept growing by listening to his instructors, coworkers, and employers, making him better at what he did. Lance lived STRONG, and as a result, he is experiencing success.

You have to live it

To start living out STRONG, begin with introspection, and ask yourself which areas you are naturally better at and which areas you need to improve. By identifying your strengths and weaknesses, you'll see which areas need a deeper focus and which areas will be easier to master.

In chapter 8, I shared that orderliness is the area of STRONG where I am weakest. Because this is my weakest area, I spend more time focusing on it. At work, I actively take time to sort and organize things. I try to prioritize tasks so I only have materials out for my highest priorities. I ask friends and family to help me stay organized. By putting a heavier focus on this area, I am managing it better than I was before.

In the same way, identify which areas of STRONG you're weakest in, and hone in on those areas as your focal points. If you struggle with teamwork, look for someone who can coach you in working with others. If you struggle with growing, find someone you trust and ask them for feedback on how you can improve yourself, then choose to welcome that feedback as a gift.

Maybe you're not working at a job right now. It's still a great time to work on becoming STRONG. Each of the STRONG skills are valuable outside employment. You'll be a better friend if you can practice being a better teammate. Being reliable will open doors for you in your personal life as effectively as it will at work. Every area of STRONG can benefit you, on or off the job.

STRONG can also be helpful as you search for employment. When you apply for a job, tell the interviewer about your soft skills, and be sure to list the skills you've learned in STRONG on your résumé. Employers love seeing employees with soft skills, and telling them that you read books on soft skills and practice them will go a long way toward helping you find employment.

Don't forget the foundation

While STRONG consists of the skills you need to find success, don't forget the foundation for success that we laid out in chapters 1-3. If you want the lessons of STRONG to take root in your life, you need to establish a mission, find mentors, and have a success-oriented mentality.

Now, head back to chapter 1 and look at your mission. What do you think of it now? Does it still line up with who you are and who you want to be? If not, this is a great time to revise it.

When your mission is what you want it to be, write it out and stick it in a place where you'll see it every day. Maybe this is a computer monitor, your car's dashboard, or your bathroom mirror. Mine is on a sticky note above the monitor in my office. Look at your mission every day as a constant reminder of who you want to be.

With a mission in place, find mentors to help you live out that mission. Who can help you live out the STRONG program? Who can help you become even better than you are now? Find those people, and let them know that you want to learn from them. Again, not every mentoring relationship needs to be formal, but it is a good idea to have a few people in your life who you can meet with regularly to learn from, bounce ideas off, and ask questions. These people can help you become STRONG and shape you into a leader.

Finally, remember to have a success-oriented mentality. Times will get tough. When they do, don't quit. Push yourself to keep going. Choose to remain positive. Remind yourself that you are worth the effort to press on and persevere. The ability to show grit – that is, to persevere in difficult times – is one of the most universal personality traits of those who achieve success. Pick any successful person you know, and ask yourself what they did when things were difficult. The answer, almost universally, is that they kept pressing forward.

This is not the end

As this book draws to a close, I want to ask one thing of you: don't let this be the end. Don't close this book and let the ideas inside fade away. Practice the lessons you've learned. Read this book again and again if you need to refresh or learn new lessons. Read other books on soft skills and personal success. Make yourself an expert at improving yourself. Change your life for the better. Fight for your success. Get STRONG. I'm rooting for you.

Study Companion
to STRONG life skills

Making STRONG work for you

STRONG life skills is an excellent program with the potential to change your life for the better. To get the most out of it, work through the following pages to make the lessons more likely to stick, ready for when you need them most. The goal behind this companion is to make STRONG work for you by asking thought-provoking questions based on the material from the book.

When to use the study companion

You can complete this companion during your first time through the book, though I highly encourage you to read the book once before you begin answering the questions. However you choose to do it, take your time and put serious thought into your answers. From time to time there will be an exercise for you to try. Don't skip these exercises – they'll help you grow!

How to navigate the study companion

You'll find section headings in the study companion to match those in the book. Read through that section from the book, then work through the coordinating section in this guide. While some of the questions and exercises will require you to read the coordinating section of the book, most are looking for your own insights.

Everything is better with mentors

Do you have a mentor yet? If not, I highly encourage you to find one and to go through this study guide with their support. Unlike schoolwork that you have to answer on your own, this homework is actually better when you "cheat" and talk with a mentor about the answers. Having an outside view can be a big help when you're trying to improve your life. Additionally, if you yourself are a mentor to someone else, go over this book with them. It could help them find their own success!

Chapter 1 – You need a mission

Success doesn't come easy

Why do you think social media influencers are so popular?

Think about a favorite social media influencer, celebrity, or athlete. Who is it? What are some aspects of their work ethic that may have helped them achieve their current status?

Success isn't always riches and fame

How do you personally define success?

Why do you think it's important to have "a mission, a mentor, and a mentality" in your life?

What is a mission, anyway?

How do you define a mission, and how does your definition differ from the one given in this section?

Gotta have goals

What is the difference between a goal and a mission?

What are some examples of short-term goals in your life?

What are some examples of long-term goals in your life?

Being SMART with your goals

What SMART goal did you set while reading this section? If you didn't set one yet, think of one now.

Your mission: more than a goal

What are a few ways defining a mission for your life can benefit you?

Look up the mission statement of a successful business you admire. How does their mission align with how you've observed their operation?

Do I *really* need a personal mission statement?

Why is it important for you to have a personal mission statement?

Ingredients for a good mission statement
List the three important characteristics in a personal mission statement.

What mission statement did you create for your life?

Consider your life as it is now. How does it align with your mission statement? In what ways doesn't it align?

Packing goals into your mission

List some of the long-term goals that will help you live out your mission.

What are a few short-term goals that fit into each of those long-term goals?

Side quests

What are some of your personal "side quests?"

How can allowing yourself time for hobbies and other activities help you accomplish your mission?

Putting it all together

Why do you think it's important to revise your mission as time goes by?

Chapter 2 – You need a mentor

What is a mentor?

How do you define a mentor? How does your definition align with or differ from the definition in this section?

Do you have anyone in your life already mentoring you? If so, how has their mentoring helped you?

Why mentors matter

According to this section, why is it important to have mentors?

How can a mentor personally benefit you?

Mentors come in all shapes and sizes

What are the benefits of a more formal mentoring relationship?

What are the benefits of a more informal mentoring relationship?

You need multiple mentors

Why is it important to have more than one mentor in your life?

What are some specific areas of your life where having a mentor would benefit you?

Finding a mentor

What are the three criteria of a good mentor?

Brainstorm a list of people in your life who might benefit you as a mentor.

Mentors make you a problem-solver

Why is it important to be a problem-solver?

Mentored goals and missions

Why is it a good thing when a mentor gives you feedback that's difficult to hear?

Exercise: If you have a mentor, take your new mission statement from Chapter 1 to them, ask their opinion, and discuss it.

Chapter 3 – You need a mentality

The most important part

How does having a success-oriented mentality make a difference?

Think like a success story

What are the negative consequences to focusing on your failures instead of successes?

Think about your mentor. (If you don't have a mentor yet, think of someone in your life who you look up to.) What are some characteristics of that person that you want in your own life?

Embrace change

Why do you think it's important to be able to make changes in your life?

What are a few areas in your life where you've said "I can't" or have struggled to change?

How can changing something help you get unstuck?

See failure as a gift

What are some ways you handle failure?

Denying that we failed

Why is living in denial about failure potentially dangerous?

Has denying failure ever negatively impacted your life? If so, how did you recover from that situation?

Anger over failure

How can anger make change difficult?

Embracing failure

What is the biggest benefit to you of learning to embrace failure?

The power of positivity

What are some of the benefits of positivity listed in this section?
What other benefits can you (or your mentor) think of?

What steps can you take to start transforming your mindset to be more positive?

Gotta have grit

How do you define grit?

How does having grit help you get ahead?

Be excellent to each other

Why is it important to create a culture of camaraderie around you?

Be STRONG

What are the six component areas of STRONG life skills?

S –

T –

R –

O –

N –

G –

How can incorporating components of STRONG into your life benefit your mentality?

Putting it all together

Which of the three foundational elements of the program (having a mission, a mentor, and a mentality) will be the most challenging for you and why? How can you make strides to overcome these difficulties?

Chapter 4 – An introduction to STRONG life skills

Time to get STRONG

What are soft skills? How are they different from hard skills?

Why do you think it's important to have a well-developed set of soft skills?

You CAN learn soft skills

Why do many employers believe soft skills can't be taught?

How to learn STRONG life skills

Can you list the six components of STRONG life skills from memory? Write them here.

S –

T –

R –

O –

N –

G –

Chapter 5 – Safety

Being STRONG starts with safety

Why is safety an important part of success?

Everything in moderation

What are some activities you enjoy that involve risk? How do you manage your safety when participating in these activities?

Safety in several settings

What are the three areas of safety in the STRONG program?

Occupational safety

What are some potential safety risks at your workplace? (If you don't work at a job right now, consider a hands-on class or activity you participate in.)

What are some ways that you can improve your safety while at work?

Why is it important for managers and business leaders to invest in the safety of their employees?

Personal safety

What does it mean to be in a safe place? How can you maintain a level of safety if there are dangers in your area?

What makes personal boundaries important?

Technological safety

Consider how much of your personal life is visible online. How can you make improvements, if needed?

Why do you think people lose hundreds of millions of dollars every year due to online scams?

Why is it important to you to practice good online security?

Putting it all together

How do occupational, personal, and technological safety overlap each other in your life?

Chapter 6 – Teamwork

The winning strategy

How do you define teamwork?

Think about the three foundation pieces for success – a mission, a mentor, and a mentality. How does teamwork help you in these three areas?

You're always on a team

What are some of the teams that you're on, and what are your roles on these teams?

Think of a time you had to take on a project by yourself. How did your project impact or influence others?

How to be a great teammate

In what ways are you a good teammate? What steps can you take to become a better teammate?

Interpersonal skills

What do you see as the biggest benefit to having good interpersonal skills?

Active listening

Think of a specific time you used active listening as described in this section. (If you can't think of a time, go out and practice active listening with someone before answering.)

How did active listening help your conversation?

Do people respond differently to active listening than passive listening? How does the response differ?

Spoken communication

Exercise: Find a mirror and give a short speech to yourself. (If you're feeling brave, find a mentor or friend and give them the speech.) During the talk, practice the tips from this section of the book.

How did your speech feel? Are there aspects of your spoken communication that you want to work on?

Nonverbal communication

What body language habits do you have when talking to others? Which are positive and which are negative?

How can you improve your body language?

Written communication

How does your professional written communication differ from your casual written communication?

Why would it be important not to use slang or shorthand in professional writing?

Emotional intelligence

Think of a time when you didn't practice emotional intelligence. What could you do differently in a similar situation the future?

How can practicing emotional intelligence help you achieve success?

Empathy

Why do you think it's important to practice empathy for others?

Acceptance

Think about a time you were able to accept a person or a situation. How was being accepting beneficial to you? How did acceptance benefit the other person or the situation ?

Conflict resolution

What are your strengths and weaknesses in the area of conflict resolution? What are some steps you can take to improve at resolving conflict?

Problem-solving

Exercise: Think of a current problem or difficult situation in your life. Using the SODAS method laid out in this section, come up with a solution.

Do you think your solution is something you'll actually do? If not, what could you do to make the solution more achievable?

Why is problem solving one of the most important skills you can learn in life?

How can you further improve your ability to problem-solve?

Customer service skills

When have you received poor customer service? How did it make you feel? What do you wish was done differently?

What does good customer service tell someone about your business?

Initiative

Think about a time when you took initiative. How did it help the situation?

Other important aspects of being a good teammate

What is "the golden rule," and why is it an important aspect of being a good teammate?

Chapter 7 – Reliability

Be there when you're needed

Why do you think hiring managers would consider the soft skill of being reliable more important than hard skills specific to the position they're filling?

How can showing up late for school or work impact others beside yourself?

Defining reliability

What is your definition of reliable? How is it similar to the definition given in this section of the book?

When was a time you were negatively impacted by someone else's lack of reliability? What happened as a result of the other person being unreliable?

Time management

What do you do well with your time management? What areas of your time management need improvement?

Planning for the unexpected

Why is it important to allot a little extra time when planning your activities?

Good time management helps everyone

What are some of the consequences of poor time management that can impact other people?

Scheduling

Do you have a schedule or calendar? If so, how does it work for you? If not, take the first step right now to start.

Prioritizing

Exercise: Write out your current list of tasks, then using the prioritization tips in this section of the book, break them down into A, B, C, and D lists.

What reasons did you have for putting items on the "A" list?

Are there items on your "D" list that you'd be better off letting go of? Why did these items make it onto this list?

Multitasking

How effective are you at multitasking? What can you do to improve your multitasking abilities?

Giving your best effort

Think about a time when you put your best effort into something. How did this make you feel?

Why would a hiring manager be interested in someone who gives their best effort?

Keeping your word

Think about a time when someone broke their word to you. What were the negative consequences in that situation?

How can keeping your word help you find success?

Communicate

How does good communication help in a business setting?

Project management

What skills that have already been covered in this book will help you with project management?

What are some of your personal traits and skills that could help you succeed in managing projects?

Working independently

Think about a time you worked independently. What went well? What do you want to do differently next time?

Why do you think it's important to own your mistakes when working independently?

Finishing what you started

What are the consequences when you abandon a project?

Becoming a leader

Why is it important to be a leader, even if you aren't in a leadership role?

Are there people who look up to you or follow your lead? What impact can you have on them by practicing good leadership? What would be the consequences of practicing poor leadership?

Chapter 8 – Orderliness

Beautiful chaos

What areas of the STRONG program do you feel you'll struggle with more? What can you do to improve your chances of success in those areas?

I get by with a little help from my friends

Who are some friends or family who could support you in being STRONG? What areas of STRONG can they help you with?

What is orderliness?

How do you define orderliness? How does your definition compare to the definitions given in this section?

Why is orderliness one of the most important soft skills you can master?

Sorting

What are some challenges you face while sorting? How can you overcome them?

Let it go

Do you have any possessions in your life that make you feel weighed down? What would be the long-term benefit of letting go?

What are some things in your life that you could easily give up?

Long-term storage

What are some things in your life that either belong in long-term storage or are already in long-term storage?

A place for everything

Why is it important to plan for extra space when storing items?

Everything in its place

How did you organize the list in this section of the book? Why did you feel that was the best system to organize these items?

Have you ever worked with someone who had a different way of organizing things from how you'd do it? How did their system differ from your preferred method?

What could be a benefit from working within someone else's organization system, even if you feel your own method would be more efficient?

Sort often

What steps can you take to develop sorting into a regular habit?

Daily orderliness

How do you practice orderliness on a daily basis?

Planning ahead

Why is it important to consider the steps of a project before you set out to do it?

Focusing

What things most distract your focus? What are some ways to manage those distractions?

Picking up

What is the danger in the workplace if you don't pick up after yourself?

Maintenance

What are the benefits of regularly maintaining your workspace?

Orderliness ties into everything

How does being orderly tie into the other areas of the STRONG program? How can being orderly make each of the other areas of STRONG better?

Chapter 9 – Noticing

Notice *and* act

Have you ever experienced the "bystander effect?" What happened in the situation?

Why is it important to act on what you notice?

Take initiative

What are the two parts of noticing in the STRONG program? Why are both important?

What does it mean to take initiative?

What to notice

What could be a more useful answer to the question "What should you notice?" than simply saying "everything?"

Notice the work that needs to be done

Why do managers find it important to hire people who take initiative?

Notice the fine details

Think about a situation when someone made a mistake in the fine details. How did it negatively impact the situation?

Notice things that can be improved

What are some things in your home or work that could be improved? How can you take initiative to make them better?

Notice opportunities for growth and advancement

If your employer offers benefits, what are some of those that you can take advantage of to better yourself?

Notice roadblocks to success

What are some potential roadblocks to your success, and what's your plan to navigate around them?

Notice others doing well

How can recognizing others doing well benefit you?

Notice others who need assistance

Why is it important to offer assistance to someone in need?

Noticing leads to growth

How can noticing (and acting on what you notice) help you grow as a person?

Chapter 10 – Growing

Last but not least

How does growing tie into every other component of the STRONG program?

How can being a person who is able to grow lead to success?

Lance's story

If you were to write a success story like Lance's about someone you know, who would it be? What part does willingness to grow play in their story?

What are a few lessons you want to remember from Lance's story?

Grow or die

Why do you think refusal to grow leads to failure?

Pick one of the businesses from this section of the book to research. How did its lack of growth lead to failure?

What are some real consequences you could face if you refuse to grow?

Learning to grow

As you read through the next section, come back here to list each of the eight skills to help you grow. What other skills can you think of that will help bring growth?

Be a self-starter

Are you a self-starter? If so, what works well for you? If you need improvement, what areas can you work on?

Be self-motivated

Why is it important to have grit and to push through challenges?

Introspection

Exercise: Think about an area of your life that you want to improve. Follow the steps in this section to practice introspection on that area.

What improvements can introspection lead to in your life?

Think of something you want to change. What can you do to give yourself an extra boost of motivation to make that change?

Critical thinking

Think of a situation in your life where critical thinking made a difference. How did critical thinking improve the situation?

Patience

Why is patience a difficult skill to develop?

What can you do to become a more patient person?

Initiative

How can taking initiative help you grow as a person?

Accepting feedback

Think of a recent time you received feedback. Was it easy or hard to hear? Was the feedback valid? How did you take the feedback?

Think about the phrase "feedback is a gift." What does that mean?

Leadership

Why is leadership important for personal and professional growth?

Authenticity

Have you ever been around someone who seems "fake?" How did they make you feel?

What are steps you can take in your life to ensure you're being authentic?

Mentoring

What are the benefits of mentoring others?

Delegation

How does delegation develop you into a leader? How does it develop others into being leaders?

Reading

Other than this book, what is a book you've read lately? How did reading that book benefit you as a person?

Exercise: Ask a mentor to recommend an article or book to help you grow.

Worth the effort

What areas of growing are difficult for you? Why is it beneficial to keep working on those areas anyway?

What are a few ways you can begin bettering yourself? Choose one to start on right away. (Consider using problem-solving, setting SMART goals from Chapter 1, and consulting your mentor.)

Chapter 11 – STRONG wherever you are

Take STRONG with you

How can practicing the STRONG program help you find success?

You have to live it

What areas of the STRONG program will you need to work the hardest to develop?

Which skills from the STRONG program do you expect to benefit you the most in your current or future employment?

Don't forget the foundation

How can STRONG help you live out the mission you established in Chapter 1 of this book?

Do you have a mentor who can help you live out STRONG skills? If so, who are they and how can they help? If not, where could you start your search for this sort of mentor?

What steps can you take to develop a mentality for success?

This is not the end

Exercise: Go back through the book and choose five sections that will benefit you in day-to-day life. Mark these pages so they're easy to find. Set this book where you'll see it often and remember to review those five sections.

Now, give yourself a pat on the back for working through the entire study companion! You're getting STRONG. Keep it up!

Skills Index
Start here when you need to find a skill

STRONG life skills consists of 60 different skills that can help you find success. The following index will help you track down those skills in the book when you need them.

STRONG
LIFE SKILLS

Lay a STRONG foundation with:

A MISSION
A MENTOR
A MENTALITY

Get STRONG by practicing:

SAFETY
TEAMWORK
RELIABILITY
ORDERLINESS
NOTICING
GROWING

ABOUT THE AUTHOR

Jim Clements began developing the STRONG life skills program in 2016, conducting more than 30 STRONG life skills workshops for more than 500 teens and young adults.

In 2018, Jim founded Made New Makerspace, a non-profit organization in Omaha, Nebraska, that has supported thousands of teens and young adults. Its mission is to empower foster and underserved youth for their success in a community that promotes learning, collaboration, and creation.

Prior to launching Made New, Jim taught high school skilled trades classes, worked as a crisis counselor, and ran a group home for underserved teens.

Jim and his wife Chelsea have served as foster parents, caring for many young people in their home through the years, and eventually adopted two of those foster children.

Jim's personal mission is to use his gifts and abilities to make the world a better place.

www.ingramcontent.com/pod-product-compliance
Lightning Source LLC
Chambersburg PA
CBHW060532130626
46553CB00002B/720